Do Central Banks Serve
the People?

Peter Dietsch
François Claveau
Clément Fontan

———————

Do Central Banks
Serve the People?

polity

First published in 2018 by Polity Press

Polity Press
65 Bridge Street
Cambridge CB2 1UR, UK

Polity Press
101 Station Landing
Suite 300
Medford, MA 02155, USA

ISBN-13: 978-1-5095-2576-8
ISBN-13: 978-1-5095-2577-5(pb)

A catalogue record for this book is available from the British Library.

Library of Congress Cataloging-in-Publication Data

Names: Dietsch, Peter, author. | Claveau, François, author. | Fontan, Clément.
Title: Do central banks serve the people? / Peter Dietsch, François Claveau, Clément Fontan.
Description: Cambridge, UK ; Medford, MA : Polity Press, 2018. | Series: The future of capitalism | Includes bibliographical references and index.
Identifiers: LCCN 2018001627 (print) | LCCN 2018002716 (ebook) | ISBN 9781509525805 (Epub) | ISBN 9781509525768 (hbk) | ISBN 9781509525775 (pbk)
Subjects: LCSH: Banks and banking, Central. | Monetary policy. | Banks and banking--Customer services.
Classification: LCC HG1811 (ebook) | LCC HG1811 .D545 2018 (print) | DDC 332.1/1--dc23
LC record available at https://lccn.loc.gov/2018001627

Typeset in 11 on 15 Sabon by
Servis Filmsetting Ltd, Stockport, Cheshire
Printed and bound in the UK by Clays Ltd, Elcograf S.p.A.

For further information on Polity, visit our website: politybooks.com

Contents

Acknowledgements

We are grateful to numerous colleagues for providing feedback on this project. Special thanks go to Romain Baeriswyl, Benjamin Braun, Boudewijn de Bruin, Josep Ferret Mas, Randall Germain and Pierre Monnin. Previous versions of the manuscript were presented at the Chaire Hoover at the Université catholique de Louvain-la-Neuve, Erasmus Universiteit Rotterdam, University of Gothenburg, McGill University, Ottawa University and at the Centre de recherche en éthique (CRE) in Montreal – thank you to all participants in these events. We also thank Jérémie Dion for his invaluable research assistance. Finally, we are grateful for the comments from two anonymous referees as well as from our editor at Polity, George Owers. This research has been supported by the Social Sciences and Humanities Research Council of Canada

Acknowledgements

(SSHRC), the Canada Research Chairs Program, the Fonds de Recherche du Québec – Société et Culture (FRQSC), and the Wallenberg Foundation.

Introduction: Central Banks Ought to Serve the People

Central banks today could not make it any clearer: their sole legitimate purpose is to serve the public interest. Janet L. Yellen, chair of the US Federal Reserve until February 2018, states that '[i]n every phase of our work and decisionmaking, we consider the well-being of the American people and the prosperity of our nation'.[1] Mark Carney, Governor of the Bank of England, refers back to the 1694 Charter for the 'timeless mission' of his institution: 'its original purpose was to "promote the publick Good and Benefit of our People..."'.[2]

In the same 2014 speech, Carney emphasises that what it means to serve the people has shifted over time: 'In 1694 promoting the good of the people meant financing a war with France.'[3] In light of the events since the onset of the financial crisis in 2007, it appears that what serving the people entails is

1

shifting yet again. Indeed, over the last ten years, central banks have moved into previously uncharted territory with policy measures such as quantitative easing (QE). These measures have inflated the balance sheets of major central banks – by five times for the Federal Reserve and the European Central Bank, and by more than ten times for the Bank of England – and radically changed the role they play in our economies. Christian Noyer, then governor of the Banque de France, acknowledged in 2014 that central banks became 'the only game in town'[4] as they took on more and more responsibilities to stabilise volatile and risky financial systems.

In this shifting landscape, can we be confident that what central banks do, and what they are asked to do, best serve the people? In particular, do central banks sufficiently take into account the side effects of their unconventional measures? Do they do enough to avoid another financial crisis? Should we trust central bankers when they intervene as experts in public debates? These are the questions at the heart of this book.

Situated at the interface between governments and financial markets, central banks are one cog in a complex institutional machinery, which has been built over the years to regulate the economy and promote the public interest. The functions given to this cog and its interactions with various other parts of the machinery have changed significantly over time. The current thinking about how central banks should serve the people mostly conforms to a template that spread like wildfire throughout the world in the 1990s. This template prescribes that the central bank should have narrow regulatory goals – archetypally limited to price stability – and that it should not coordinate with other parts of the machinery, especially not with the legislative and executive branches of the State.

This book is built on the premise that an in-depth evaluation of the role of central banks in society should not take this template as given. The increased importance of monetary policy in the macro-economic toolkit since 2007 confers additional importance to this project. Our main contribution lies in defending the claim that, on three matters, central banks today do not seem to best serve the people in their monetary zone. In Chapter 2, we maintain that the inegalitarian effects of monetary policy since the 2007 crisis are worrisome, and that the arguments for disregarding them when formulating monetary policy are dubious. In Chapter 3, we argue that the current institutional configuration is favouring the interests of the financial sector at the expense of the broader public interest. In

Chapter 4, we diagnose a conflict of interest inside central banks between two types of expertise they produce, which undermines the trust we can have in the information they provide on some topics. With these three concerns in mind, the concluding chapter indicates an array of policy alternatives that could make central banks better servants of the public.

Two conditions must be in place to productively discuss how central banks can best serve the people in the future. First, participants in the discussion must understand how central banking works. The next chapter aims to supply the essential elements of such an understanding to non-specialist readers. Second, participants must be ready to seriously entertain the possibility that the current institutional configuration is not optimal. This condition does not seem to be met today among the specialists on central banking, that is, professional economists. Ninety-four per cent of economists who participated in a recent survey agreed that 'it is desirable to maintain central bank independence in the future' – 'central bank independence' being the phrase used among specialists to describe how the central bank as a cog currently relates to other parts of the institutional machinery.[5] This book argues that this conventional wisdom needs to be revisited

Introduction

in light of the recent dramatic changes both in how the financial side of a modern economy works and concerning the policy instruments employed by central banks.

1

Central Banking: The Essentials

In this preliminary chapter, we aim to provide enough information about the workings of central banking for a non-specialist audience to be able to follow our subsequent discussion.

The characteristic that singles out the central bank among all of the institutions in a currency area is that it has a monopoly over the issuance of legal tender. It is not the only institution that 'creates money' – in fact, commercial banks are the principal creators of money today – but central bank money has a special status: it is the ultimate form of settlement between economic agents. All other monies (for instance, the sum that is credited to your bank account when you contract a loan) are promises ultimately redeemable in central bank money.

This monopoly puts the central bank in a favourable position to pursue two goals that a society is likely to have: financial stability and price stability. First, it can intervene at moments of financial turmoil to act as a lender of last resort because it can create liquidity without constraints. Second, it can contribute to a stable price level by manipulating the price of credit. Although central banks have at times had various other roles (promoting employment, managing the exchange rate and the national debt, supervising financial institutions, etc.), the goals of financial stability and price stability are constantly present. Note that, for the sake of clarity and brevity, this book focuses on three central banks, namely the European Central Bank (ECB), the Federal Reserve (Fed) and the Bank of England (BofE).

In addition to the extent of their mandates, a changing characteristic of central banks has been their degree of coordination with other state actors, especially with elected officials. Before the 1990s, governments typically had considerable direct influence on monetary policy. Things have changed with the worldwide generalisation in the 1990s of a template known as 'Central Bank Independence' (CBI).[1] The next section discusses what central banking was like under this template. With the 2007 financial crisis, central banking has changed yet again – these changes are introduced in the second section of the chapter. In both sections, we have to get into somewhat technical discussions about the instruments of monetary policy. We keep the technicalities to the bare minimum needed to follow the arguments of the rest of the book.

There is also a general lesson to be learned from this chapter. The breadth of the mandate of central banks and their degree of coordination with other state actors are two variables that, historically, have been positively correlated. In other words, the typical pattern is: the higher the degree of independence of central banks, the smaller their set of goals.[2] As we will see, the CBI template respected this pattern, but the current situation does not.

The Central Bank Independence era

The CBI template calls for various protections to ensure that central banks are not subject to 'political' pressures in setting their monetary policy. We will discuss the theoretical underpinnings of this prescription at length in the next chapter. For now, the following should suffice: the general worry is that, without a high degree of independence, central bankers might not be credible to market participants when stating that they are thoroughly committed to fight inflation. Markets might think that politicians will veto a hawkish monetary policy because they fear lower short-term economic growth, higher costs of servicing public debt, and the impact these might have on their chances of winning elections.

Even with laws prohibiting elected officials from directly telling central bankers what to do, one might worry that politicians could still exert strong indirect pressures by threatening them with funding cuts. But this trick cannot work with central banks because, unlike most other public agencies, they generate their own income (from the interest on liquidity lent and the returns on their financial assets). Consequently, the distance from political influence created by implementing the CBI template is real.

The CBI template not only promoted a high degree of independence of central banks, it also defined their mandate narrowly by historical standards. The main task of central banks became price stability. The focus on one objective follows the historical pattern associating a high degree of independence with narrow mandates, but a further element is needed to understand why price stability became in effect the only item on the agenda. What happened to the goal of financial stability? As

Chapter 3 will discuss, financial stability was put on the back burner because of the belief – widespread before the 2007 financial crisis – that modern financial technology together with price stability would be sufficient to greatly moderate credit cycles.

When observed from the perspective of how the basic institutions of society 'hang together as one system of cooperation',[3] the CBI template stands out as implying that central banks must not consider how their policies contribute to societal objectives beyond price stability. Other institutions, including government, must take monetary policy as a given and optimise accordingly when promoting other societal goals, such as limiting economic inequalities (see Chapter 2). Under the CBI template, there is little to no coordination between monetary policy and other policy levers.

With this general picture in mind, we need to understand how monetary policy has actually worked since the 1990s. Central banks aim to nudge the general price level upward at a low and steady pace – the target of a 2 per cent rate of inflation being the norm. They do not directly control the myriad of prices in an economy – those are set by countless decisions of economic agents – but monetary policy has an indirect impact on prices through various 'channels of transmission'.

Central Banking: The Essentials

In the media, we usually hear about central banks 'raising' or 'lowering' interest rates. How exactly does this process work? Even though the institutional details vary from central bank to central bank, every central bank identifies a 'target rate'. In the case of the Fed, for example, the target rate is the federal funds rate, that is, the rate that banks charge each other for overnight loans on the interbank lending market. A lower target rate will incentivise commercial banks to charge lower interest rates to their customers for consumption loans or mortgages. A higher target rate does the opposite. These changing credit costs to economic agents make them modify their investment and consumption decisions, which in turn change the level of inflationary pressures on the economy.

The instruments central banks typically use to influence the target rate are called Open Market Operations (OMOs). They build on the fact that commercial banks need liquidity to settle their day-to-day transactions with each other. Commercial banks can get liquidity from the central bank, but they do not necessarily have to – they can also turn to each other. Indeed, they typically roll over their debt on the interbank lending market. To influence interest rates on this market, the central bank must change how easily commercial banks can access liquidity. This is where OMOs come in. Think of a central bank as a bankers' bank: it provides liquidity to commercial banks against specific assets that act as collateral. Suppose the central bank intends to *inject* liquidity; in this case, it will acquire assets from commercial banks, using central bank reserves that are credited to commercial banks' accounts. OMOs usually come with a repurchase agreement, that is, the central bank will sell back the assets at a later date, and the liquidity will be returned with interest. By way of illustration, OMOs function in a similar way to pawnshops: liquidity is provided against collateral when economic agents need it. In the CBI era, the duration of typical exchanges was short (usually a week).

In addition, central banks not only affect economic variables (notably the price level) through OMOs, they also have an impact by virtue of publicly announcing their plans. Speeches by central bankers are particularly effective in influencing behaviour because they shape the *expectations* of market participants.

In sum, in the CBI era, central banks had a direct lever on short-term credit to commercial banks (via OMOs) and indirect but reliable effects on longer-term credit to all market participants (thanks to adjustments by commercial banks and to changes in expectations). Given how monetary policy worked in this era, we can understand why it was broadly perceived as apolitical: it was easily interpreted as a purely technical matter where the goal is both narrow and consensual and the means to attain it benign.

Central banking after 2007

Since the 2007 financial crisis, the interventions of central banks in advanced economies have expanded beyond the CBI template: central banks now play a more significant role both in financial and, as we shall see in subsequent chapters, in political systems. Yet, the degree of coordination of central banks with other state actors has remained low. In a recent survey of central bank governors worldwide, only two out of fifty-four respondents asserted that 'Central bank independence was "lost a little" or "lost a lot" during the crisis.'[4] The current situation thus departs from the general historical pattern where a broader set of goals should go with less political isolation. What happened to central banks?

Let us start with the 2007 financial crisis. In the summer of 2007, the interbank lending market froze: commercial banks stopped lending to each other because they could no longer assess the trustworthiness of their counterparts – astronomic amounts of dodgy financial products were on their balance sheets. One year later, within months of the failure of Lehman Brothers and the US government's bailout of AIG, the monetary policy of the Fed effectively hit the zero lower bound and was unable to lower interest rates further. Central banks thus turned to unconventional measures in order, initially, to restore confidence on the interbank lending market and prevent a financial meltdown and, subsequently, to reboot the economy.

More specifically, they modified and extended OMOs using two kinds of system-wide intervention. First, OMOs were extended in size, range of collateral, length. These measures include the well-known Long-Term Refinancing Operations (LTRO) of the ECB, which we will examine in depth in Chapter 3. Second, central banks launched quantitative easing (QE) programmes, that is, the outright purchase – as opposed to repurchase agreements – of large amounts of financial assets on secondary markets. Under these programmes, central banks have purchased a wide range of financial assets from institutional investors. These assets vary in maturity and include government bonds, asset-backed securities and corporate securities.

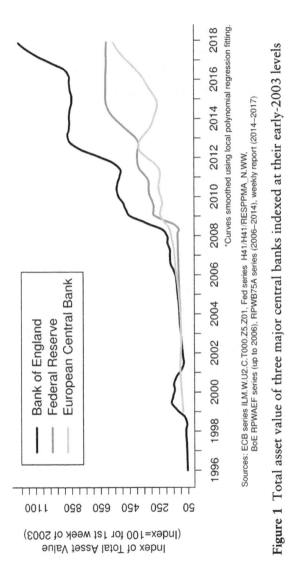

Sources: ECB series ILM.W.U2.C.T000.Z5.Z01, Fed series H41/H41/RESPPMA_N.WW, BoE RPWAEF series (up to 2006), RPWB75A series (2006–2014), weekly report (2014–2017)

*Curves smoothed using local polynomial regression fitting.

Figure 1 Total asset value of three major central banks indexed at their early-2003 levels

Thus, central bank policies clearly have become more important than they were prior to the crisis, as is illustrated in Figure 1 by the growth in the total value of assets held by major central banks. As a result of this intensive use of their balance sheets (instead of concentrating on setting short-term interest rates), central bankers have increased their intermediation role in the economy and, according to many, have been increasingly straying into the political realm.

These system-wide interventions were 'novel' only to a degree. First, the Bank of Japan had been using QE since March 2001; this policy instrument was thus not invented in response to the crisis. The experience of the Bank of Japan should make us pause: at the time of writing, it is still pumping liquidity in the system through QE and the value of its total assets is reaching astronomical amounts, especially since the launch of an even more aggressive policy in October 2013.[5] The Fed has recently taken the first steps towards unwinding its balance sheet, but it remains too early to tell whether this policy will be successful. Extrapolating from the first three months of unwinding, its balance sheet will be back to the level of 2008 only in 2072. Second, the 'new' interventions use the old channels:[6] monetary policy is still transmitted through financial markets. Under extended OMOs, the central bank still exchanges liquidity with commercial banks in exchange for financial assets. Under QE, the central bank still tries to affect economic activity through interest rates, although it now targets long-term rates directly instead of the short-term rates on the interbank lending market.

In addition to these changes in monetary policy, central banks have also obtained financial supervision competences, which they had not held since the end of the 1990s. More specifically, both the ECB and the BofE have added or expanded roles in micro- and macroprudential supervision. They now have the power of supervising individual financial institutions as well as of controlling systemic risks. In the case of the ECB, the expansion of another type of influence has been particularly drastic: it exerts a direct pressure on Eurozone economic reforms through the conditionality of its financial interventions and its participation in the so-called 'troika', which includes the European Commission and the International Monetary Fund beside the ECB.[7]

In sum, since the start of the financial crisis in 2007, central banks have moved beyond the narrow role assigned to them by the CBI template.[8] Central banking has entered a 'new era' in which the certainties associated with the CBI model no longer apply.[9] Among these lost certainties is the belief that maintaining price stability by setting interest rates is an apolitical, technical task, which suffices for ensuring financial stability. This also puts pressure on the idea that the formulation of monetary policy is best left to highly skilled technocrats isolated from democratic institutions. Among members of the central banking community and of the financial elite, this reconsideration of the place of central banks in the institutional machinery is broadly seen as a 'threat to central bank independence'. For instance, the Group of Thirty, a 'consultative group' composed of central bankers, leading financiers and academic economists, is worried:

> Unfortunately, since the crisis began, increasing attention has been drawn to the fact that many of the policies that central banks have followed do have clear distributional implications. This has invited increased government scrutiny of what central banks do, thus constituting a threat to central bank independence.[10]

In the next chapter, we discuss precisely this concern about the distributional implications of recent central bank policies, albeit without the status quo bias expressed by the Group of Thirty.

2

Central Banking and Inequalities

Suppose you fall ill and your doctor prescribes you a drug to cure you from your affliction. If the drug in question has known side effects, you will expect your doctor to take these unintended consequences of the treatment into account and weigh them against its intended benefits. If your doctor failed to do this, you would not be happy.

Monetary policy has unintended consequences, too. Central banks cannot target price stability, financial stability or employment in isolation and without affecting other policy objectives. Notably, monetary policy has an important impact on the distribution of income and wealth. This impact has become more pronounced with the unconventional policies employed since the financial crisis. Mark Carney, the governor of the BofE, for example, acknowledges that 'the distributional consequences of the response to the financial crisis have been significant'.[1]

It might seem obvious that central banks should take the unintended consequences of their policies into account. Why do they not? First, they state that this is not their job. As Benoît Coeuré, a member of the board of the ECB, puts it, taking into account inequalities 'is not the mandate of the ECB, or of any modern central bank'.[2] This, however, begs the question, because the analogy to the doctor suggests precisely that it might be a mistake not to include a reference to inequalities in central bank mandates. Second, defenders of narrow central bank mandates centred on price stability (and maximally including employment and financial stability) also have more substantive reasons for their position. They point out, on the one hand, that sensitivity to inequality makes for a less effective monetary policy and, on the other hand, that it would be inappropriate to ask unelected, apolitical institutions such as central banks to make distributive choices that are deeply political. These considerations underpin the CBI template described in Chapter 1.

On closer inspection, the second of these lines of response once again begs the question. It takes as given the current institutional structure of independent central banks with a narrow mandate. Yet, what about alternative institutional arrangements? What about, for instance, central banks with a wider mandate including sensitivity to inequalities and a corresponding framework of stronger political control? Granted, under their current, narrow mandate, central bankers cannot be blamed for neglecting the distributive consequences of their actions. However, we *can* criticise a lack of openness and imagination for alternative institutional arrangements when the *status quo* has serious shortcomings. The increased politicisation of monetary policy is a fact, not a choice. As a society, we need to deliberate about how to respond to this fact.

The other line of response – that making monetary policy sensitive to inequalities would reduce its effectiveness – presents a more fundamental challenge that calls for a detailed response. Providing such a response is the goal of this chapter.

We shall start with a short primer on the importance of caring about inequality. Especially in monetary policy circles, the concern for inequality is often misunderstood, and so it is important to clarify what underpins this concern. In a second step, we present the available evidence for the impact of monetary policy on inequalities, particularly since the financial crisis. These elements will lead us to the intermediate conclusion that a more integrationist stance is called for vis-à-vis different policy objectives such as the traditional goals of monetary policy on the one hand, and distributive concerns on the other. We will then present an important challenge to this view. The economic literature on monetary policy might be interpreted as suggesting that making monetary policy sensitive to distributive concerns will necessarily be suboptimal. The assessment of the so-called time-inconsistency argument underpinning this claim lies at the core of the chapter. We conclude that while it indeed identifies an important and relevant consideration for monetary policy, it does not undermine our claim that monetary policy should be sensitive to distributive concerns.

Why care about inequalities?

Policy objectives need to be underpinned by a justification that explains why they are important. Without such a justification, it is impossible to know what weight the objective in question should receive compared to other goals.

For instance, in the case of monetary policy, why is low and stable inflation a goal worth pursuing?

Several reasons are usually cited in response, let us just focus on two of them here.[3] First, inflation represents a tax on nominal assets – that is, assets not indexed to inflation. If you have $1,000 in your bank account and inflation is at 5 per cent, then after a year the real value of your money will fall to just over $952. This implicit tax, so economists argue, leads to inefficiencies in the allocation of resources. Second, fluctuations in the rate of inflation, which historically tend to be larger at higher rates of inflation, create uncertainty and thus undermine investment. Note that all of the justifications for the desirability of low inflation are *instrumental* in nature: low and stable inflation is a good thing, because its absence will undermine other social values or objectives.

Similarly, why and to what extent should we care about economic inequalities? First, it is important to stress that we care about inequality not merely because excessive inequalities undermine the pursuit of other policy objectives, but because we consider that containing inequalities is a worthy goal for its own sake. In other words, and in contrast to inflation, inequality matters for intrinsic and not just for instrumental reasons.

Yet, the concern central bankers show for inequality usually remains limited to instrumental considerations. They will accept the need to contain inequality if they believe that inequality undermines monetary policy objectives such as employment or financial stability. By contrast, as we have shown in a discourse analysis of central bankers published in previous work,[4] most central banks do not attribute intrinsic value to containing inequalities. And even in the rare cases where they do, they point to their narrow mandate to argue that promoting this intrinsic value is not their job. Let us emphasise again that, given their current mandate, it might be too harsh to blame central bankers for this omission. But, as a society, we cannot afford to leave these trade-offs unaddressed. This is like the doctor ignoring the side effects of the drug he prescribes you. Understanding and resolving these difficult trade-offs is precisely what we expect our various government agencies to do.

Second, note that limiting *inequality* does not entail striving for *equality*. Instead, the task of theories of justice is to formulate a criterion that allows us to assess what kinds and what magnitude of inequalities are justified. Containing inequalities is worthwhile for its own sake only up to the point where the remaining inequalities are legitimate from the perspective of justice. The further we are from a just distribution, the more urgent the need to reduce inequalities. To illustrate, consider an example of a theory that formulates such a criterion. John Rawls argues that inequalities are justified to the extent that they better the position of the least-advantaged members of society.[5] Both his and other prominent theories of justice are compatible with substantive socioeconomic inequalities.

Importantly, we do not need to endorse any particular such theory for the purposes of our argument in this chapter. Most theories of justice today agree that the current level of socioeconomic inequality is excessive. Even libertarians would accept that a significant proportion of today's inequalities does not stem from the free and voluntary interactions of individuals but from past injustices. Moreover, both economic research, such as Thomas Piketty's seminal analysis, and the platforms of most political parties also share the consensus view that today's inequalities are excessive. Against this background, if it is the case that monetary policy exacerbates these inequalities further, then this will obviously be problematic. It is to this demonstration that we now turn.

Do Central Banks Serve the People?

The distributive impact of monetary policy

'[A]ny monetary policy will have some distributional impacts. But if monetary policy actions could be vetoed so long as someone was made worse off then there could be no monetary policy.'[6] Before the 2007 financial crisis, this kind of reasoning underpinned the conventional wisdom that while monetary policy had distributive implications, these were minor, unsystematic and inevitable, and therefore not worth getting worked up about. If this view was controversial even in pre-crisis times, it is certainly no longer tenable today.

With interest rates quickly hitting the zero lower bound after the crisis, central banks turned to unconventional monetary policies. At the heart of these unconventional policies lie the QE programmes described in Chapter 1. It turns out that these massive purchases of financial assets affect distribution in several ways. As a result, neglecting the distributive impact of monetary policy is no longer an option. In this section, we will document two specific transmission channels from QE to distributive outcomes. This analysis is not meant to be exhaustive – there are likely to be others, such as the cross-border impact of monetary policy, which we bracket here. We will also assess and reject the objection raised by many central bankers that the distributive consequences of QE had to be tolerated because any alternative policy would have produced even more inequality. So how exactly does QE affect distribution?

(1) First, and most importantly, consider the impact QE has on inequalities in income and wealth via its substantial injection of liquidity into the economy. By employing QE, central banks hope to affect inflation and spending through several channels, most of which also entail an impact on inequality. Here, we concentrate on one of these channels, namely the so-called *portfolio balance effect*.[7] Central banks pay for the assets they purchase under QE through the creation of central bank reserves. The institutional investors that sell the assets now have cash on their books instead of the assets they held initially. 'They will therefore want to rebalance their portfolios, for example by using the new deposits to buy higher-yielding assets such as bonds and shares issued by companies.'[8] Higher demand for a vast class of assets will push up their prices and, subsequently, is expected both to stimulate spending through a wealth effect and to stimulate investment by lowering the borrowing costs for corporations.

However, whether reality lives up to these

expectations of economic theory depends on the answer to one crucial question: What is the additional liquidity provided by QE used for?[9] There are two basic options: productive investment *versus* investment in existing financial assets. The portfolio balance effect will only have the desired effect if the additional liquidity actually feeds through to productive investment. Unfortunately, in times of economic crisis, this is particularly unlikely. The valuable insight of John Maynard Keynes' notion of the 'liquidity trap' is that investment depends largely on investor confidence rather than on available liquidity. Hence, it is to be expected that additional liquidity will be ineffective to stimulate investment. Think about it: if investors are reluctant to invest in the real economy with interest rates already at the zero lower bound, under what circumstances, if any, would extra liquidity be sufficient to change their mind?

When business confidence is low, both the initial injection of liquidity through QE and the second-round wealth effects are thus more likely to lead to investment in existing financial assets rather than to productive investment. This is of course not to say that QE will not have *any* stimulating effect on the real economy, but it is plausible to think that the desired effect will be small compared to the amount of liquidity injected.

This expectation is borne out by most empirical analyses of the distributive impact of QE. Whether it is academic experts, the Bank of International Settlements, or central banks themselves, there is an overwhelming consensus

a) that QE led to a boom on asset markets such as stock exchanges and real estate – for example, in the ten at first disastrous and then rather lack-lustre years in terms of economic growth since 2007, the Dow Jones index has risen steadily from its low of below 8,000 points to above 25,000 in March 2018; and

b) that this boom has exacerbated inequalities by benefiting the holders of these assets, who tend to be already privileged members of society – for example, one influential study estimates that in the US the top 1 per cent captured 91 per cent of income gains in 2009–12.[10]

Even if one accepts that there are some countervailing factors,[11] and even if the causal relationships are too complex to determine what percentage of asset price rises is due to QE, it is fair to say that the inegalitarian impact of QE is real and significant.

However, this is not the end of the story quite yet. There are many who, while agreeing with the above consensus, argue that a world without QE would have been worse for *all* members of society. QE was necessary, so they claim, to avert financial meltdown, a scenario that would have hit the poor and disadvantaged members of society even harder and made them worse off compared to a world of QE. In short, defenders of this position maintain that *there is no alternative* (TINA).

Granted, QE was preferable to doing nothing. However, the TINA argument does not fly.[12] In response to the crisis, central banks did not seriously consider alternative policies that could have achieved their monetary policy objectives of price stability, financial stability and employment *without* generating the above unintended distributive consequences. Why not a 'helicopter drop', for instance, a direct deposit of money in citizens' bank accounts? This would have required significantly less liquidity compared to QE in order to produce the same stimulus. Central banks can hardly claim that injecting hundreds of billions of dollars, pounds sterling or euros through QE is less radical a measure than injecting tens of billions via a helicopter drop.[13] Given the central banks' preparedness to reach for extraordinary and innovative measures in response to the crisis, why not choose ones that cause less collateral damage in terms of inequalities? If they once again point to their mandate as an excuse, this merely proves our point that the narrow mandate is problematic from a broader perspective that takes into account wider policy objectives.

(2) We now turn, albeit more briefly, to a second way in which QE affects distributive outcomes. It matters not only *that* central banks are buying financial assets under QE, but it matters also *which* assets they buy. As already mentioned, QE has heralded an expansion of the asset classes included in central bank purchasing programmes. In particular, many central banks have included corporate bonds (and shares, in some cases) in their QE programmes. The ECB's corporate sector purchase programme (CSPP) represents one of the most recent examples. If you buy the bonds of a firm, so the argument runs, this will lower its borrowing costs and thus stimulate investment. Note that the distributive concern one might have here, namely the preferential treatment of some corporate interests, differs from the worry emphasised earlier that QE will increase inequalities in income and wealth.

Independently of whether more investment actually results (see the reservations expressed earlier), there is no doubt that being included in these purchases confers an advantage on the firms in question. Volkswagen, for example, having been locked out of bond markets in the wake of its emissions scandal, was able to return to the markets thanks to being included in the ECB's programme.[14] How do central banks decide which firms to include in these programmes? The ECB's response to this question appeals to market neutrality and argues that it aims to buy a basket of corporate bonds that is representative of the market.

Yet, neutrality among corporations that issue bonds does not imply neutrality among all firms operating in the economy. It favours corporations that are active on the bond market and tends to exclude small and medium-sized enterprises, for instance. Thus, a corporate bond buying programme of this type amounts to a kind of hidden industrial policy with a distributive impact. Moreover, once we recognise that neutrality is elusive, why not endorse the political nature of corporate bond buying schemes and use it to promote other political objectives. For example, why not use QE to reduce the carbon-intensity of our economies?[15] Why not exclude arms producers such as Thales from the ECB's programme? The appeal to neutrality cannot hide the fact that corporate bond purchasing programmes are deeply political operations with distributive implications that stretch beyond the boundaries of the narrow mandates of central banks.

The intuitive solution

In light of the above demonstration that the pursuit of monetary policy objectives narrowly defined creates collateral damage in distributive terms, it is plausible to think that a better integration of different policy objectives is called for. When we speak of integration, we have in mind the identification and promotion of the overall policy mix that best serves the people or what economists call the social welfare function. Who would disagree with that, you might ask? Well, as we have just seen, the current division of institutional labour does not contain a mechanism to include the unintended distributional consequences of monetary policy in policy design.

The integration of policy objectives necessarily involves trade-offs. For example, we might be prepared to accept a slightly higher level of inflation in exchange for a significantly less inegalitarian distributive outcome; conversely, we might accept a moderate increase in inequality if this allows us to significantly reduce inflation.

Importantly, this does not imply that we should let *one* government agency take all policy decisions. There exist both informational constraints – a planned economy does not work – and concerns of political domination – such a concentration of power is never a good idea – against such a model. Therefore, a division of institutional labour is needed and should be preserved. When it comes to integration of the standard goals of monetary policy and other policy objectives,[16] there are two basic models. One can either officially maintain the current, narrow mandate of central banks, but put in place channels of communication and coordination between them and other government agencies, fiscal authorities in particular, to avoid the policies of one undercutting the mission of another. Alternatively, one can ask central banks themselves to actively pursue a wider set of policy objectives, e.g. distributive concerns. Since their mandate would include politically charged topics, their democratic accountability should be promoted through a mix of *prior* precise specifications of the mandate and *subsequent* political control relying on parliamentary hearings or other instruments. We shall come back to these two basic options in Chapter 5. In any case, when adjusting the mandate, one will also need to make sure that central banks dispose of the adequate instruments to promote multiple objectives.

Central Banking and Inequalities

The challenge to integration of policy objectives

Some economist readers might be shaking their head in despair at this point. Have the authors not understood the argument, they might ask, that lies at the heart of the case for an independent central bank with a narrow mandate? Do they not realise that integration of policy objectives will invite inflationary bias, thus making monetary policy less effective? Any call for more integration does indeed have to take these questions seriously. Yet, we will now show that this challenge does not in fact undermine our call for more integration of policy objectives.

To begin with, it is imperative to distinguish two potential sources of inflationary bias. We will see that these two sources nicely map onto the development of the literature on central banks over the last fifty years. Their discussion, in non-technical terms, thus offers the additional benefit of gaining an understanding of the theoretical trajectory leading to the CBI template that dominates thinking about central banks today. Recall that CBI has two central aspects: independence on the one hand, and a narrow mandate of price stability on the other.

(1) First, the classic public choice argument for an independent central bank is the following:[17]

politicians will always be tempted to use monetary policy for electoral purposes. An increase in the money supply usually gives a temporary boost in output before this effect is neutralised by rising wages and general price inflation. Politicians will thus tend to increase the money supply before elections, trying to fool voters into believing that their policies have led to permanent economic growth. A well-known example of these tactics is the 9 per cent increase in the US money supply in 1972, which is believed to have stemmed from a deal between President Nixon and the formally independent Federal Reserve.

Several comments on the public choice view: first, the concerns about the political instrumentalisation of monetary policy should indeed be taken seriously when thinking about the integration of policy objectives. However, they have to be balanced against the costs of a lack of integration, which we emphasise here.

Second, whereas the public choice argument certainly deserves praise for drawing our attention to the interests of elected policy makers, it would be equally naive to presume that central bankers do not have interests of their own. To give but one illustration, in the wake of the sovereign-debt crisis in Europe, the ECB has been accused on several occasions of attempting to extend its influence without having the formal mandate to do so. Think of its role in the troika and its fixing of the bailout terms for Greece, for instance.[18]

Third, making central banks independent might be part of a strategy by governments to avoid being blamed for unpopular political decisions. Think of the contractionary monetary policy of the Fed under Chairman Volcker, which put the spotlight on the central bank rather than the White House and Congress.[19]

In sum, from a public choice perspective, the case *for* independence when it comes to price stability has to be weighed against the case *against* independence for broader reasons of accountability. The outcome of this balancing act is not a foregone conclusion.

(2) Let us turn to the second potential source of inflationary bias and the argument that has been central in underpinning the CBI template. We should note up front that this argument is built on the premise of a double mandate of controlling inflation and employment; in other words, it refers to the American context and the mandate of the Fed. However, the conclusions from this argument are applied to central banks generally.

Once we have decided to hand monetary policy to an independent central bank with a double mandate of controlling inflation and promoting employment, this institution faces incentives to use inflation surprises, that is, a more expansionary than anticipated monetary policy, to attempt to lower unemployment. However, doing so leads to higher than optimal inflation. The central problem here is one of time inconsistency.[20] Let us unpack this claim.

There are three key elements to the basic version of the time inconsistency argument: its premises, the suboptimal result that flows from these premises, and the policy upshot. The first premise of the time inconsistency model is wage rigidity, that is, the fact that economic agents enter into wage contracts that cannot be immediately renegotiated when the economic environment changes. Under wage rigidity, the central bank will be tempted to expand the money supply in an inflation surprise, because this will temporarily make it cheaper in *real* terms to hire workers, thus promoting employment as the central bank's mandate dictates.

The second premise of the model is that economic agents are rational. They will anticipate the inflation surprise and base their wage negotiations on the higher rate of inflation in the first place. Hence, the overall suboptimal result is higher than necessary inflation without unemployment being any lower.

Finally, what is the policy upshot of all this? This first, classic version of the time inconsistency argument concludes that discretionary monetary policy setting is not *credible* and should be replaced by monetary *rules*. By adopting a rule rather than relying on discretionary monetary policy making, so the argument runs, central banks will convince economic agents to lower their inflation expectations. A monetarist rule of a constant growth of the money supply *à la* Milton Friedman or the Taylor rule both represent examples for such a rule.[21]

Now, it is not clear why this argument would speak against making monetary policy sensitive to distributive concerns. After all, the monetary policy rule could simply be extended to include distributive objectives or constraints.[22]

However, once again, this is not quite the end of the story. Two types of counterarguments can and have been made to put the time inconsistency argument into perspective. To begin with, notice that it is not at all clear why the conditions that generate time inconsistency in the economic model obtain in the real world. For example, some have challenged the strong rationality assumption behind the rational expectations framework. Others have pointed out that time inconsistency would disappear if wage contracts were concluded in real rather than nominal terms. Finally, it is not obvious why central banks, if truly independent, would persistently aim to lower unemployment below a level that is sustainable. Even staunch defenders of the CBI paradigm such as the former chief economist of the ECB, Otmar Issing, seem to recognise this point and the fact that, if it holds, the problem of time inconsistency will simply disappear.[23] From this perspective, as Alan Blinder eloquently put it, in pursuing the time inconsistency problem, 'academic economists have been barking loudly up the wrong tree'.[24]

For the sake of argument, however, let us grant that time inconsistency is indeed a real phenomenon, and turn to the second way in which it has been challenged. The general idea here can be summed up by saying that rule-based monetary policy will in some situations lead to the non-pursuit of reasonable stabilisation policies and thus end up producing intolerably high levels of unemployment.

How can we get around this problem? Is there a way to have our cake and eat it too, that is, can we have a central bank that succeeds in convincing economic agents of its general anti-inflation stance while still according some weight to employment considerations? The answer is the 'Rogoff central banker', named after the economist Kenneth

Rogoff. Rogoff's idea is that if we appoint a central banker who is known to be more conservative than the public at large, which means that he accords *more* weight to price stability than to employment compared to the public at large, the resulting policy mix will indeed be optimal.[25] That is, it will avoid both a lack of credibility and the resulting time inconsistency problem, while preserving the discretion in monetary policy making that the rule-based approach lacks. Only central bankers with a credible anti-inflation bias will be able to attain the optimal equilibrium between price stability and other objectives. If their commitment to low inflation is not credible, this will generate 'unnecessary' inflationary expectations and move us away from the optimal policy mix. If there is one idea in central banking circles that has been elevated to a quasi-religious status and taken to conclusively justify the CBI template, it is Rogoff's.

However, it is premature to think that Rogoff's argument justifies CBI. 'Indeed, the main insight of Rogoff, so frequently cited simply in support of independence, should be seen as being to reject too firm a commitment to price stability.'[26] Even a hawkish central bank, if it takes seriously the inflation-employment trade-off, will in some circumstances accept small increases in inflation for substantial gains in employment. More generally, 'in the design of a monetary constitution, society faces a trade-off between credibility and flexibility: strong incentives for the central bank to achieve price stability may result in unnecessary losses in terms of other economic variables'.[27]

This is grist to our mill because *distribution represents one of these variables*. If a central bank takes seriously the distributive consequences of certain kinds of monetary policy, it will in some cases choose *some* deviation from its inflation target to avoid generating substantial inequalities. Arguably, the strongly inegalitarian QE policies fall into this category: avoiding some of these inequalities at the cost of some price or financial stability might well have been worth it.

Thus, rather than presenting an argument *against* the integration of policy objectives, Rogoff's argument in fact *calls for* integration. Central bankers face a dilemma: *either* they accept Rogoff's argumentative structure, in which case they should also accept our case for more policy integration, and for some distribution-sensitivity of monetary policy; *or* they reject Rogoff, but in this case one of the central planks of CBI goes out the window, too.

One last comeback of defenders of an independent central bank narrowly focusing on price stability has been mounted on empirical grounds. Alesina and Summers argued in the 1990s that 'while central bank independence promotes price stability, it has no measurable impact on real economic performance'.[28] This line of argument denies the existence of trade-offs between price stability and employment. Two comments are in order on this result in our context. First, times have changed, and it would be interesting to see whether this result still holds today. Second, and more fundamentally, these findings are limited to the trade-off between price stability and employment, and tell us nothing about the trade-off between price stability and distributive outcomes that concerns us here.

In sum, the Rogoff-variant of the time inconsistency argument and the argument from credibility both recognise that integration of policy objectives involves two potential costs: (1) the potential costs in terms of higher inflation that stem from economic agents believing that the central bank is less inflation-averse than it actually is; (2) the potential costs in terms of other policy objectives that stem from the central bank according too much weight to the objective of price stability. The CBI paradigm focuses almost exclusively on the former cost, while ignoring the latter. This has dramatic consequences.

Conclusion

Faced with the enormous literature on the optimal institutional design of monetary policy, it is easy to lose sight of the forest for all the trees.

Let us sum up how our argument for making monetary policy sensitive to distributive considerations relates to the theoretical underpinnings of CBI. First, it is useful to distinguish the public choice argument, which exclusively addresses questions of independence, from the time inconsistency argument, which addresses wider issues related to the central bank mandate. Second, the public choice argument is far from conclusive. Third, the initial formulation of the time inconsistency debate (by Kydland and Prescott) was a red herring – today, most people accept that some discretion is needed for optimal monetary policy. That said, a rule-based monetary policy is in principle compatible with taking into account distributive concerns. Fourth, the argument that best represents the conventional wisdom on central bank mandates today (Rogoff) recognises the need for a certain integration of policy objectives and thus does not necessarily call for a narrow mandate. The bigger the collateral damage of monetary policy in terms of other policy objectives, the stronger the argument for integration.

If, as the second section of this chapter has argued, the collateral damage of QE in terms of inequality is significant, this is indeed an argument for more integration of policy objectives. The challenge to our argument has been rebutted. For central banks to effectively serve the people in modern economies such as ours, more integration is required. More specifically, a monetary policy that is blind to its distributive consequences will not serve the interests of the population well.

3

Central Banking and Finance

The evolution of global financial markets in recent decades has affected central banks in a paradoxical fashion.[1] On the one hand, financial markets empower central bankers to the extent that political elites rely on them to manage global market pressures. For example, during the Eurozone crisis, the influence and the power of the ECB on the formulation of EU member states' economic policies has grown considerably, in part due to its expertise on financial issues. On the other hand, larger, interconnected and highly leveraged financial systems threaten the power of central bankers because systemic financial crises are more likely. Since central banks are supposed to ensure financial stability, their reputation and their autonomy are at risk when financial crises occur.

In light of this paradox, how do central banks

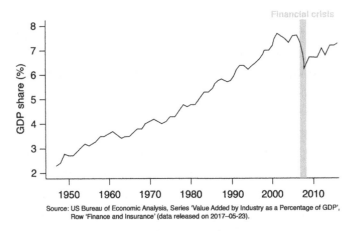

Source: US Bureau of Economic Analysis, Series 'Value Added by Industry as a Percentage of GDP', Row 'Finance and Insurance' (data released on 2017-05-23).

Figure 2 GDP share of the financial sector in the United States, which has tripled since the late 1940s

relate to financial developments? Are they prudent supervisors of financial markets or failed regulators? Are they able to ensure that our societies will benefit from financial innovation or do financial market pressures undermine their capacity to steer the economy?

Since the mid-1980s, the process of financialisation has driven the most decisive changes in the financial sector, and maybe in the economy as a whole.[2] Financialisation is defined as the growth of the financial sector vis-à-vis the non-financial sector (see Figure 2) and the increasing dependence of the non-financial sector on financial logic – for example, the growing importance of shareholder value in the operations of firms. Central bankers were amongst the fiercest supporters of the financialisation of the banking sector, promoting financial innovations such as derivatives and securitisation. This support stands in stark contrast to the usual description of austere and conservative central bankers, who are supposed to reduce liquidity when the animal spirits on financial markets run high. The first part of this chapter exposes the central bankers' positive beliefs about, and strategic interests in, financialisation before the 2007 global financial crisis.

After that crisis, one might have expected central bankers to revise their position on financialisation, as it became clear it had fuelled the sudden liquidity crisis in August 2007 and the bankruptcy of Lehman Brothers in September 2008. Had the crisis not clearly shown that financialisation fails to align private financial interests with public welfare? Far from a change of paradigm in the financial world, our societies have witnessed the resilience of problematic financial activities and powerful financial institutions.[3] Post-crisis central banking has contributed to this resilience to the extent that its unconventional monetary policies mainly aim at fixing short-term problems such as risks of financial collapse or lacklustre growth, rather than addressing middle- and long-term concerns such as the reining in of unduly risky financial activities. The second section of the chapter explains this lack of control with the concept of financial dominance.

Central banking and the pre-crisis financialisation of the banking sector

A model commercial bank is a patient institution that relies on its local knowledge to make money by playing the role of intermediary between savers and borrowers. A classic example of this model are the banks traditionally serving the German *Mittelstand* of small and medium-sized enterprises. However, banks have progressively moved away from this business model since the mid-1980s. In fact, it would be impossible to understand the pre-crisis relationship between central banks and the commercial banking sector without taking into account the evolution of the latter towards market-based banking.[4]

Market-based banking is a central component of the financialisation process, and has been driven by financial innovation and financial deregulation. It increases the pressure of market imperatives on non-financial companies and reinforces the pro-cyclical dynamics on financial markets. For our purposes, two aspects of market-based banking matter. First, on the asset side of the balance sheet, banks rely on an 'originate-to-distribute' business model, that is, they make loans with the intention of selling them to other investors, rather than holding the loans until they mature. Second, on the liability side of the balance sheet, banking activities are increasingly relocated in over-the-counter repo markets, where banks pawn their assets at other financial institutions for short-term loans. The transactions taking place on repo markets are repurchase agreements, where one party agrees to buy a specific security and to sell it back at a later date and at a predetermined price. The spread between the two prices represents the interest paid to the creditor. Banks increasingly rely on repo markets because they can borrow more money at a lower cost compared to interbank lending markets. The figures speak for themselves: the transactions taking place on EU repo markets reached €25 trillion annually in 2008, almost double the volume of the transactions on interbank lending markets.[5]

In the next two sections, we document how the Fed and the ECB supported the development of market-based banking before the crisis. In particular, we explore the ideas and incentives that led them to underestimate the risks associated with market-based activities such as derivatives trading, securitisation and the transactions taking place on repo markets.

The idea side: why do central bankers believe in market-based banking?

Under market-based banking, financial markets and banks are closely intertwined. Before the financial crisis, the vast majority of regulators, academics and central bankers perceived this association to be beneficial, because they believed that more complete and integrated markets would strengthen the stability of the whole economic system and boost its efficiency in allocating resources. From this perspective, financial regulation is superfluous at best and perhaps even undesirable, as it risks undermining market liquidity.

However, from a historical point of view, the deregulation and resulting expansion of financial activities tend to produce financial instability rather than stability. Finance is cyclical and alternates between phases of mania followed by moments of panic when the overly optimistic beliefs underpinning the mania collapse.[6] Credit expansion (notably in the housing market), growing balance sheets of banks, and speculative bubbles characterise phases of mania.

Given that the build-up of financial imbalances in the early 2000s was quite similar to previous phases of financial mania, why did regulators and central bankers not anticipate the subprime speculative bubble? The short answer is that they believed the numerous financial innovations of the 1990s had effectively tamed systemic financial risk. They were not alarmed about the likelihood of a financial crisis because they believed that historical conditions had changed, that 'this time [was] different'.[7] In particular, regulators and central bankers praised securitisation and derivative markets because they were supposed to make financial markets more resilient. For example, at the 2007 Jackson Hole meeting of central bankers, Ben Bernanke compared these innovations to those of the New Deal.[8] However, as it turned out, increased securitisation and derivatives trading played a central role in the subprime crisis.[9]

Securitisation refers to the process by which separate loans or other financial assets are combined into a single financial instrument and subsequently sold to investors. By bundling relatively safe and relatively risky loans, securitisation was supposed to lower the risk associated with the ownership of debt obligations. More specifically, mortgage-backed securities (MBS) were designed to spread the ownership of risk from mortgage lending in the United States. The model ran into trouble for three reasons. First, MBS increased the risks of irresponsible lending because lenders who plan to pass on the asset have fewer incentives to check the ability of the borrower to service their mortgage. Second, MBS ignored 'tail risks', that is, the possibility of a collapse of the whole US housing market. Third, even though the MBS market was a small part of the US financial system, it considerably enhanced the scope for systemic risk, because the financial products were purchased by many financial institutions inside and outside the US. When MBS losses started to materialise, financial institutions had to sell other financial assets at fire-sale prices in order to compensate for these losses, triggering the 2007–8 downward price spiral.

Derivatives are bets between two market participants on asset price movements. They were created to hedge against risks related to asset price fluctuations. Almost non-existent in 1980, the derivatives market was worth $500 trillion in June 2007, about ten times the value of global GDP. This spectacular growth shows that derivative contracts became increasingly disconnected from real economic activity. A specific form of derivatives, credit default swaps (CDS), which were often used for speculative reasons, mainly fuelled this expansion. A CDS allows you to bet on, and hence hedge against, the default of someone else's loan, including mortgages. Against a premium, a CDS issuer will offer to pick up the bill in case the loan turns sour. CDS lulled investors and financial institutions into a false sense of security, because they thought these instruments protected them against potential losses from other assets, including MBS. Moreover, the balance sheets of financial institutions often did not report the amount of CDS, because they were traded through offshore Special Purpose Vehicles. This opacity allowed financial institutions, such as the US insurer AIG, to take massive and risky bets on the CDS markets without alarming its counterparts. When the MBS market collapsed, CDS issuers such as AIG were overwhelmed by the financial obligations they faced due to losing these bets.

As these innovations extended market activities and made them allegedly more stable and efficient, most central bankers, albeit to different degrees, considered financial regulation superfluous. For example, Jean-Claude Trichet, the former ECB President (2003–11), promoted the self-regulation of markets as the best regulatory option until at least October

2007. In October 2008, a US senator reminded Alan Greenspan, Chairman of the Fed from 1987 to 2006, that he once stated: 'I do have an ideology. My judgement is that free, competitive markets are by far the unrivalled way to organise economies. We've tried regulation. None meaningfully worked.'[10] Because central bankers believed in self-correcting markets, they also claimed that monetary policy should not 'lean against the wind' by counteracting the formation of asset prices bubbles. Leaning against the wind is one of the oldest central banking doctrines. In violation of this maxim, Alan Greenspan and Ben Bernanke developed a doctrine of 'benign neglect', calling for central banks to focus exclusively on their inflation target and not on asset prices. As late as 2005, Greenspan stated that it was simply not realistic to believe policy makers could reliably diagnose speculative asset bubbles when they form. Instead, he maintained that markets would adjust automatically, that is, market operators would systematically react against speculative bubbles and thus cause prices to revert to their fundamental levels.[11]

In short, central bankers developed a favourable bias towards financial expansion because they wrongly believed that it would make financial markets more stable and efficient. Consequently, central banks did not 'lean against the wind' and paid little or no attention to the early signs of the subprime crisis.

The interest side: what do central bankers gain from the expansion of financial markets?

While they are certainly important, it would give economic ideas undue weight to consider them as the sole explanatory factor for central bankers' support of financialisation. In addition to the considerations just discussed, central bankers have come to consider financialisation as a phenomenon that enhances the effectiveness of monetary policy. On some occasions, they have even developed policy instruments conducive to the spread of market-based banking. While this strategy was hailed as a success before the crisis, the downside was that central bankers progressively lost control over the credit and financial expansion that led to the 2007 crisis. Let us consider the Fed and the ECB in turn.

Since the 1980s, the Fed has struggled to contain inflation while avoiding responsibility for the social costs attached to anti-inflationary policies.[12] When Paul Volcker was Chairman, the Fed took harsh measures to get a grip on inflation. These measures had a contractionary effect on the economy, and the Fed faced severe criticism from Congress and from economic lobby groups such as farmers and car dealers. The latter mailed in coffins containing the car keys of unsold vehicles. After this episode, the Fed realised that the combination of deepening bond markets and increasing the transparency of its monetary decisions could potentially help steer the economy in a more indirect way, thus avoiding some of the blame for unpopular policies. How so? With the financialisation of the US economy, asset prices had become an important determinant not only of investor confidence, but of the economic outlook more generally. Thus, when the Fed hinted at the future course of monetary policy – a process later dubbed forward guidance – markets immediately priced in these changes, triggering a feedback to the real economy before the Fed had actually done anything. In some instances, this self-fulfilling prophecy proved so effective that the Fed did not even have to follow through with a previously announced policy change because it had become unnecessary. At the same time, Fed policy makers shielded themselves from potential criticism by claiming that their policy adjustments were merely following and validating movements on financial markets.

However, there was a catch 22. As the Fed needed liquid and stable markets to pursue this strategy, it ended up providing an implicit guarantee against sharp market decline, also known as the Greenspan put. This opened the door for a serious problem of moral hazard on the markets. Since investors knew that the Fed relied on them for its monetary policy and would lower interest rates when the markets hit a bump, they took excessive risks in the early 2000s.[13] At the time, concerns were brushed aside, and the Fed strategy even received regular praise. Greenspan was often called a 'magician' or 'maestro', because the combination of low inflation and buoyant economic activity propelled by credit expansion helped the Fed achieve its dual mandate. Yet, the strategy was at odds with the idea of 'leaning against the wind'. As the Fed increasingly followed market movements and expectations, it did not engage in any significant countercyclical tightening of monetary policy during the boom. The markets did not auto-correct against the formation of the US subprime speculative bubble, and the Fed in fact 'validated' this lack of attention by keeping interest rates low. In sum, the reliance of the Fed on financial markets' expectations to implement its monetary policy was conducive to soaring asset prices and contributed to the subprime crisis.

As for the ECB, it also relied on the growth of financial markets during the first decade of its existence, but for different reasons. Because of the financial and economic heterogeneity of the Eurozone area, ECB policy makers feared that their monetary policy would be impaired. First, financial heterogeneity threatened to diminish the ECB's control over interbank lending rates in different countries and thus to undermine the transmission channel of monetary policy to the real economy. Second, the fact that the business cycles of different member states were not aligned made it impossible to find a single interest rate that would be appropriate for all of them at the same time. Think for instance of the contrast between booming Ireland and the stagnant German economy of the early 2000s. The ECB and the European Commission promoted the idea of a unified European repo market as a solution for the financial and economic fragmentation of the Eurozone area. As with many other areas of European integration, unification meant that different national repo markets were liberalised in a similar fashion. The hope was that, with such a unified repo market, demand for sovereign bonds would increase, interbank lending rates across the Eurozone would converge, and national business cycles would become more strongly correlated.[14]

To pursue this agenda, the ECB adjusted its own collateral frameworks to mirror those that had been put in place by the 2002 Financial Collateral Directive. Following these changes, government debt obligations from all Eurozone countries were increasingly considered as identical collateral on repo markets. In other words, if you were a bank looking for short-term financing, your Greek bond would have exactly the same value as your German bond, say, at least in terms of collateral.

At first sight, the policy achieved one of its two objectives. Since financial institutions now had an incentive to invest heavily in peripheral Eurozone bonds – they were cheaper than French, German or Dutch bonds, but treated as identical in repo transactions with the ECB – they drove up their prices. This lowered the yield on these bonds and led to an artificial convergence of interest rates across the Eurozone. However, the policy also had an important unintended side effect. Mirroring a Eurozone repo market that tripled in size between 2001 and 2008, the balance sheets of Eurozone commercial banks more or less doubled in size between 1999 and 2007 to reach an average of 350 per cent of GDP in Eurozone member states. They became 'too big to fail'.

The ECB strategy did not achieve its second objective. The financial integration of the Eurozone did not lead to the convergence of national economies. Instead, through the mechanism just outlined, it led to substantial capital flows from the (core) Eurozone banks to (periphery) Eurozone states and households, raising the levels of public and private debt, and fuelling the build-up of financial and economic imbalances in the Eurozone. The combination of these factors set the Eurozone up for the perfect storm when the financial crisis hit. Not only were Eurozone banks cut off from the short-term funding they had become dependent on when repo markets froze, but malfunctioning repo markets also led to a sharp increase in the yields of government bonds on the Eurozone periphery. Only then did it become plain to see how the ECB, together with other political actors, had contributed to tying the economic fate of Eurozone states to the health of financial markets.

In sum, the Fed and the ECB believed that financialisation would serve both to make markets more complete (ideas) and to improve the capacity of central banks to steer the economy (interests). In addition, the Fed wanted to avoid blame for the social costs of contractionary monetary policies, and the ECB tried to foster economic integration within the Eurozone. Both of these attempts to govern the economy at a distance through financial markets came with unintended consequences, and have ultimately weakened central banks' control over those markets. The financial exuberance ignited in the early 2000s on both sides of the Atlantic unravelled abruptly in 2007 – this time was not different. Against this background, it will seem even more surprising, as we shall now see, that central banks kept relying on and supporting financialisation even after the crisis, albeit for different reasons.

Post-crisis central banking and financial dominance

Standard approaches in monetary theory predict that the liquidity central banks have injected since the crisis will impact the real economy. Appealing to these theories, both conservative monetary theorists in Germany and members of the US Republican Party have argued that the vast amounts of liquidity provided by central banks will at some point cause the economy to overheat and translate into inflationary pressures. Yet, during the ten-year period since the launch of unconventional monetary policies, these fears have not materialised. If anything, central bankers have been more concerned to avert deflation.

This section offers an explanation to this puzzle,

namely the fact that central banks are subject to financial dominance. The latter obtains when the attainment of central banks' policy goals is compromised by some contingent features of financial markets or patterns of behaviour of market participants.[15] As a result, central banks become less effective in pursuing their mission of serving the people, while financial institutions are able to game the system and obtain economic rents. For example, when central banks implement unconventional measures with the explicit goal of boosting loans to corporations, but financial institutions use this liquidity for other means, this is an instance of financial dominance.

Financial dominance is a matter of degree. The more central bank liquidity is channelled into existing assets rather than into real investment, the more monetary policy suffers from financial dominance.

In what follows, we disentangle the functional relationship between central banks and commercial banks in order to understand how financial dominance operates in the post-crisis context. More specifically, we distinguish two facets of the phenomenon. First, the capacity of central banks to boost growth and inflation in order to reach their objective of price stability is restricted by the *infrastructural power*[16] of financial markets, that is, the control that commercial banks exercise over the transmission channels of monetary policy. For example, as described in Chapter 2, quantitative easing programmes depend on the portfolio balance effect to impact the real economy. Second, the commitment of central banks to financial stability is compromised by *the power of weakness* of commercial banks that are too big to fail. For example, central banks will be tempted to bail out insolvent financial institutions for fear of the systemic consequences their failure would have. The resulting moral hazard increases the likelihood of future crises.

Infrastructural power

As financial markets form the transmission channels of monetary policy, central bankers have a vested interest in their smooth operation. In fact, under the current set-up of our financial infrastructure, central banks cannot affect the real economy without the participation of private financial institutions. Against this background, the shift from traditional banking to market-based banking unsurprisingly affects monetary policy, too. We will analyse two practical implications: first, central banks today intervene to ensure liquidity on markets prone to instability; second, they face new challenges in convincing commercial banks to use any additional liquidity in ways that will actually lead to the desired outcomes.

First, in times of crisis, central banks play an active role in the stabilisation of market segments, such as for instance repo markets or securitised financial products, whose connection to monetary policy at first sight seems remote. Why do they do this? Central bankers claim that problems on these markets will hamper the transmission of monetary policy. For example, the objective of the 2012 Outright Monetary Transactions (OMT) programme, the second programme of bond purchases by the ECB, was not only to ease speculative tensions on the sovereign bond markets of peripheral Eurozone countries. It also aimed at stabilising repo markets by providing a floor to sovereign bond prices, which are used as collateral on repo markets. The role of repo markets is so crucial for the ECB's transmission of its monetary policy that ECB representatives even oppose the EU proposal to include repo markets in a potential financial transactions tax.[17] The Fed is equally opposed to stricter regulation of repo markets.[18] Similar considerations motivate central banks today to buy securitised products and to push securitisation, often in the face of resistance from other regulators. For instance, both the ECB and the BofE have advocated policies to revive securitisation.[19] In other words, central bankers are supporting, and even promoting, the financial innovations that led to the crisis, because monetary policy has come to rely on them.

Second, there is a huge gap between an injection of liquidity by the central bank and the desired impact on the real economy. To begin with, even commercial banks that are strapped for cash might refuse to accept the liquidity offered by central banks because it comes with a stigma and sends a signal of weakness to competitors. In order to overcome the challenge posed by stigmatisation, central banks underline the systemic nature of their programmes and offer the liquidity under conditions that commercial banks will find hard to refuse. This was the explicit goal of the ECB's 2012 Long Term Refinancing Operations (LTRO). These open-market operations provided over €1 trillion of liquidity (9 per cent of the Eurozone's GDP) for the Eurozone financial system at a fixed rate of 1 per cent and under relaxed collateral requirements. European banks indeed could not resist. They swapped a number of risky assets they no longer wanted to hold, in particular bonds from the Eurozone periphery, against liquidity. Orthodox

ECB insiders argue that this transfer of (privately held) risky assets to the (public) ECB balance sheet mainly benefited the major banks based in Paris and Frankfurt.[20] Even though Mario Draghi stated that '[w]e would prefer it if they [i.e. banks] would lend the money to companies and households',[21] the ECB did not control how the banks used this liquidity. They often simply used it to buy relatively safe but higher-yielding assets, for instance other sovereign bonds, and pocketed the difference. Consequently, the liquidity created by the ECB did not help the real economy that much overall. Draghi himself acknowledged in front of the European Parliament that these financial operations were problematic.[22]

Experience also shows that when central banks attach conditions to their offers of liquidity to make them more effective, commercial banks might not play along. The ECB's targeted LTRO (TLTRO) programmes in September and December 2014 are a case in point. Under these programmes, commercial banks had to pass on a certain proportion of the borrowed liquidity to the real economy. If they did not, they would have to reimburse the liquidity before the maturity date of the loan and could not participate in subsequent offers. TLTROs were not a great success, however, as European banks were reluctant to borrow liquidity under those conditions. In March 2016, the ECB caved in and weakened the conditionality.

In sum, when they design monetary policy, central banks are constrained by the market-based banking structure of the financial system and by the interests of commercial banks. Under the current financial architecture, in order to influence real economic variables and reach their policy objectives through traditional channels of transmission, central banks find themselves compelled to stabilise and even promote the dysfunctional parts of the financial system, and to 'enrol' financial institutions to participate by appealing to their profit motive. The infrastructural power of the financial sector fuels financial dominance and leads to a monetary policy that primarily serves finance rather than society as a whole.

The power of weakness

Weakness can at times be the greatest asset of a financial institution. When you are a systemically important bank, that is, a bank whose failure would have serious repercussions throughout the financial system, then you know that the central bank in its role as lender of last resort is more likely to bail you out. This knowledge creates a problem of moral hazard. Not only are systemically important banks prone to be more careless about managing their risks – after all, the central bank is unlikely to let them fail – but any financial institution now faces an incentive to grow to a size that is considered 'too big to fail' (TBTF) and that hence invites preferential treatment from central banks. In this final section of the chapter, we assess whether central banks have done enough since the crisis to address this issue of moral hazard.

First of all, what *should* central banks do when they are faced with an insolvent bank? The classic rule of thumb, developed by Walter Bagehot in the nineteenth century, was to bail out banks suffering from a mere liquidity crunch, while letting insolvent banks fail. The former refers to a situation where your assets cover your liabilities overall, but your short-term assets are insufficient to meet your short-term liabilities; the latter refers to a situation where your assets fall short of your liabilities, period.

The phenomenon of TBTF banks complicates things, because letting a TBTF insolvent bank fail is not an option. The Bagehot rule needs to be complemented in two ways. First, together with other financial regulators, central banks should prevent commercial banks from becoming too big to fail in the first place, for instance by a relatively strict control of mergers and acquisitions in the industry. In addition, commercial banks should be forced to put funds aside for hard times. Second, when rescuing TBTF banks, central banks should attach conditions strict enough to have a deterrent effect for the future – nationalisation for example.

How does the performance of central banks since the 2007 financial crisis rate from this perspective? Here, it is useful to distinguish their immediate response on the one hand, from their crisis management in later years on the other. In 2008, the Fed implemented two bond purchasing programmes (Maiden Lane II and III) that targeted the 'subprime' market and derivative financial products to which AIG was exposed. However, there was no conditionality attached to the use of this liquidity and, in March 2009, AIG granted a highly controversial $218 million bonus payment to the employees of its financial services division. This kind of central bank policy aggravates moral hazard rather than reduces it.[23]

Now, you might want to defend the Fed by suggesting that the risks of a financial meltdown would have been too great in 2007–8 had it acted otherwise. We are sceptical about the merits of this point, because it buys into precisely the logic of moral hazard that we are trying to avoid. But, for argument's sake, let us grant it. However, note that even if this argument holds for 2007–8, it certainly *does not* hold in subsequent years when the immediate threat of a financial meltdown is over. Especially since central banks have acquired additional competences of banking supervision since the crisis, one would have expected them to take active measures to address the problem of TBTF financial institutions in its aftermath. While *some* regulatory reforms such as the creation of the banking union in Europe have recently been implemented, not enough has been done in this regard.[24] We shall come back to possible remedies in Chapter 5.

Let us conclude this section with a last observation. There is a certain irony to the fact that, when faced with a trade-off between short-term financial stability and long-term financial stability, central banks tend to favour the former. After all, this is what the policies just surveyed amount to. The irony lies in the fact that this is as clear-cut a case of time inconsistency as you are likely to find: central banks know they should not write insolvent TBTF financial institutions a blank cheque but, when the time comes, they shy away from attaching meaningful conditions to their bailouts.[25] Contrary to what one might think from a cursory look at the literature, this shows that time inconsistency can afflict central bankers just as much as politicians.

Conclusion

The monetary policies pursued by major central banks before the financial crisis were conducive to the financialisation of the economy. This trend was supported by the paradigm dominant among central bankers at the time. They believed, wrongly, that more complete markets, relying on financial innovations such as securitisation and derivatives, would make financial markets more efficient and more stable. The opposite was the case.

In addition, financialisation was popular with important central banks for reasons specific to the policy agenda they were pursuing. The Fed used the increased liquidity on financial markets to manage the economy through forward guidance, which allowed it to deflect responsibility for unpopular monetary policy measures. The ECB promoted the development of European repo markets to serve its goals of financial integration and economic harmonisation across the Eurozone.

More surprisingly, the policies of central banks since 2007 suggest that they have not fully learned the lessons from the crisis. We have explained this fact by appeal to the concept of financial dominance, which obtains when the attainment of central banks' policy goals is compromised by contingent features of financial markets or patterns of behaviour of market participants. The chapter has distinguished two aspects of financial dominance: first, the infrastructural power of commercial banks, that is, the influence they have on the effectiveness of monetary policy. Central banks are dependent on commercial banks to act in certain ways for the transmission channels of monetary policy to function. The second aspect of financial dominance is what we have called the power of weakness of TBTF financial institutions. When faced with an insolvent TBTF financial institution, central banks will be tempted to undermine their control over moral hazard and bail it out. Central banks have done surprisingly little since 2007 to reduce the likelihood of finding themselves in this situation.

In fact, the two facets of financial dominance should be considered in interaction rather than in isolation. Central bank reluctance to engage in a more heavy-handed regulatory approach can be explained at least in part by the fact that they have come to rely on the market-based banking of large financial institutions to conduct their monetary policy in an effective manner. At the same time, the infrastructural power that financial institutions hold over central banks reinforces the problem of TBTF banks.

Do Central Banks Serve the People?

In sum, these considerations lead us to conclude that future research and policy design related to central banking should worry just as much about the independence of central banks vis-à-vis financial markets as about their independence vis-à-vis governments.

4

Central Banking Expertise

Central bankers are experts: they are socially recognised as having specialised knowledge on topics such as the monetary system and financial regulation. We can divide their expertise into two types. First, they are *regulatory* experts when they make decisions, most importantly those on monetary policy. It is due to their status as regulatory experts that they are generally trusted to *know how* to implement the proper policies. Central bankers are also *testimonial* experts when they tell the general public and policy makers how the economy and central banking work and how they should work. Because their 'know-how' translates into a socially recognised 'know-that', what central bankers claim to be true of the economy is widely considered reliable information.

Central bankers' authority as testimonial experts

is impressive. Alan Greenspan is emblematic in this regard. In a 2002 Senate Committee Hearing, Senator Grimm thanked him for his regulatory expertise, claiming that the Fed's monetary policy 'has been the foundation of our economic stability'.[1] The Senator added:

> I think one of the great services you provided to this country has been the wisdom of your views and the credibility that they contain when you have been willing to speak out on issues like energy derivatives [. . .][2] [Y]our willingness, when asked, to state your opinion on an issue like that, in an era such as the one we currently are operating in, has been critically important and has had a profound effect on the policy of the Government and the country.

This attribution of testimonial expertise above and beyond regulatory expertise is not limited to Greenspan and his era. For instance, highly ranking European officials who were involved in the early phase of the Greek government-debt crisis reported in interviews that, in policy circles, 'there is the idea that if the ECB is saying [something], it is true'. One interviewee also recalls that, at a crucial moment, the 'Germans were saying "There is just one person Merkel [the Chancellor of Germany] will listen to, it is Trichet [the ECB president], nobody else."'[3]

Central Banking Expertise

In the previous chapters, we primarily examined how well central bankers serve the people in their role as regulatory experts. This chapter focuses on whether central bankers serve the people well as *testimonial* experts. Its main conclusion is that the interest of central bankers in furthering or protecting their position as *regulatory* experts is, in some important respects, in conflict with their performance as *testimonial* experts.

How to evaluate testimonial experts: a procedural framework

Central banks are fallible and they have failed us in the past. Take the belief, consensual before the 2007–8 financial crisis, that the combination of deregulation and financial innovation had led to a more stable financial system about which central banks need not worry much (see Chapter 3). We found out that this belief was dangerously wrong.[4]

Today, central bankers say that they have learned their lesson and no longer believe in the automatic stabilisation of financial markets. So, what can we conclude about their current trustworthiness as testimonial experts? Our best shot at answering this question is not to probe the justification for each of their stated beliefs – to be reliable, this strategy would require assessors who are even more knowledgeable than central bankers in their domain of expertise. The most promising strategy is to calibrate our trust by evaluating the extent to which they possess the characteristics required to effectively correct any mistaken beliefs they may hold.

Indeed, we know quite a lot about the general characteristics that foster or hinder the reliability of an expert community. We even have tales and idioms for some of these characteristics. In 'The Emperor's New Clothes' for instance, Hans Christian Andersen illustrates a damaging characteristic: if saying what is true is likely to damage one's interests, what seems true to the many risks remaining unspoken. In the tale, no one except 'a little child' dares to say that the emperor is naked, because 'that would prove him either unfit for his position, or a fool'.[5] Knowledge seeking and sharing can conflict with the protection of someone's interests.

Since the rumour in the emperor's town was that the clothes would not only exist but be made from 'splendid cloth', what the damaging characteristic really hampered was *error correction*. Everyone started from the belief that they would see magnificent garments; the conditions were not in place to collectively revise their beliefs. Similarly, what we assess in this chapter is whether the conditions for an effective error-correction mechanism are in place for central banks.

We propose to use a three-part framework to assess the quality of the error-correction mechanism.[6] The three conditions come in degrees and we have reasons to believe that an improvement in any of the dimensions increases the likelihood of error correction. The conditions are based on the premise that much of error correction happens through a social process of structured criticism. This process can be effective only if (1) the initial claims to which agents are committed are public, (2) the social context promotes rather than hinders the production of intellectual challenges to these commitments, and (3) individuals or collective agents have the proper dispositions to adjust their beliefs based on the strength of the arguments put forward. Let us say a few more words on these three conditions before turning to assessing central banks.

The first condition is one of *transparency*. To give a fair chance to 'transformative criticism',[7] incumbents must help potential challengers by stating what their beliefs are and on what grounds they think their beliefs are justified. If these two aspects are not made public, criticism is too easily dodged by either claiming that one's beliefs have been misinterpreted or by comforting oneself with the idea that the 'real' justification for one's beliefs is unscathed.

The second and most complex condition requires a social context that fosters the *sustained* generation of *varied criticism*. A criticism uttered once is unlikely to profoundly disrupt the conventional wisdom of a community; this is why it must be sustained. But challengers should not, as a group, always hit on the same nail because that implies most beliefs would go unquestioned. We need the lines of criticism to be varied.

Different characteristics of the social context have an impact on the condition of sustained and varied criticism. Most straightforwardly, direct censure limits criticism. Andersen's tale points to a more insidious characteristic: a concern to preserve one's social standing – e.g., not being perceived as unfit or a fool – can mute criticism. Since an expert gains and retains her social standing as an expert by being recognised as 'fit' in her community of specialists, pressures to conformity do exist and can inhibit criticism. Regarding the variety of criticism, a vast literature argues that such variety is promoted by having community members with varied backgrounds: members with different gender, cultural, socioeconomic, theoretical and professional backgrounds appear more likely to ask different questions, to spot unsupported assumptions, to come up with novel interpretations of data, and so forth.[8]

The third and last condition is the *modifiability of group beliefs* based on arguments. Even if transparency is high and the flow of criticism is sustained, error correction stalls if members of the community are too wedded to their prior beliefs. Political debates among established parties give a stark example of how error correction can fail to occur even if positions are public and criticism generation is working at full speed. There are two broad reasons why this condition of belief modifiability might not be met. First, recognising that one was wrong, irrespective of what one was wrong about, can have a reputational cost. Second, the content of the alternative belief can be uncomfortable. At the end of Andersen's tale, although the king 'suspected [his subjects relaying the child's observation] were right', he decides to keep acting on his prior belief – the reputational cost of recognising that he has been fooled and the discomfort of accepting that he is actually naked both contribute to his lack of responsiveness.

In the rest of this chapter, we apply this three-part

framework to assess the error-correction mechanism of central banks.

Central bankers and transparency

Central banks used to be shrouded in mystery. In December 1929, the Deputy Governor of the Bank of England, Sir Ernest Musgrave Harvey, defended the opaqueness of his institution before the Macmillan Committee charged with investigating the banking and financial systems in the aftermath of the 1929 stock market crash:

> **Committee member John Maynard Keynes:** [I]s it a practice of the Bank of England never to explain [. . .] the reasons for its policy?
> **Harvey:** It is a dangerous thing to start to give reasons.
> **Keynes:** Or to defend itself against criticism?
> **Harvey:** [. . .] As regards defence against criticism, I am afraid, though the Committee may not all agree, we do not admit there is need for defence; to defend ourselves is somewhat akin to a lady starting to defend her virtue.[9]

The situation changed radically in the course of the 1990s (yes, that late), and most if not all central banks have moved towards greater transparency by now.[10] Their websites supply large amounts of information, from the wealth of data they collect to the speeches of board members explaining their policies.

This development means that central banks meet the first condition of an effective error-correction mechanism to a higher degree today than they used to. But central banks are *conditionally* transparent and the reasons why they are more transparent today have little to do with a desire to improve error detection in their *testimonial* expertise. These reasons have a lot more to do with their desire to be effective *regulatory* experts. Consequently, we must refrain from giving them a perfect score on this first criterion.

Why are central banks more transparent today? Two reasons are emphasised in the literature and by central banks themselves. The first reason relates to concerns for democratic accountability. Central banks are given significant powers to serve the people. In return, society demands that central bankers justify what they are doing based on the goals that they should strive for. With a higher level of independence and of discretion in the choice of the means to pursue their goals, central bankers ought to be more transparent to allow a proper assessment of their actions.

Do Central Banks Serve the People?

The second reason is that the effectiveness of monetary policy is promoted by a high level of transparency, or so it is widely believed today. Central banks must manage the expectations of market participants in order to successfully play their stabilising role. Communication can be a great tool for expectation management, but it requires that central banks' verbal commitments be perceived as credible.[11] To gain and retain this credibility, central bankers have put in place intricate communication schemes through which they convince market participants that their goals are stable and consistent, that they carefully monitor the economic situation, and that they act on the incoming information in a predictable manner. As the ECB website puts it, that is how modern central banks ensure that 'price expectations are well anchored'.[12] Once credibility is well-established vis-à-vis market participants, central bankers can affect expectations of future interest rates by simply offering their own predictions (see Chapters 1 and 3).

These arguments for transparency are focused on central bankers as *regulatory* experts. But the same considerations also suggest *limits* to transparency. To further their capacity to control financial markets through words alone, central banks must have tightly policed communications. Accordingly, transcripts of policy meetings are released by only a few central banks and always after a considerable time lag.[13] These policy meetings produce carefully crafted messages, which have often been debated at the level of single word choice. As Otmar Issing puts it: 'Communication and transparency therefore [. . .] become a balancing act for the central bank, which has to assess the impact of communication on the efficiency of monetary policy.'[14]

This conditional transparency can be justified when transparency is taken as a means to increase the effectiveness of monetary policy and it can probably be tolerated on grounds of democratic accountability (because central bankers can be asked *later* to take responsibility for their actions). But there is a third function to transparency, which is not optimally served by conditional transparency: facilitating well-informed criticism generation by outsiders in the pursuit of error correction.[15] This function is conspicuously absent from the contemporary discussion of central bank transparency, but it was in fact flagged by Keynes back in 1929 when questioning Deputy Governor Harvey:

Keynes: Does not the policy of secrecy as to its intentions deprive the Bank of what I might call the collective wisdom of the community? These questions are very difficult and very novel. They require a great deal of co-operative thinking by all people who are competent to contribute to the common stock. Does not the policy of secrecy of the Bank mean that no one outside the Bank can express an opinion which is founded on sound information?

Keynes had a point: after the 1929 stock market crash as well as in the midst of the 2007 financial crisis, central bankers did not have full access to collective epistemic resources because they felt some information had to be withheld from public scrutiny. These examples indicate that their testimonial expertise is constrained by the short-term imperatives that come with their regulatory expertise.

Central bankers and criticism generation

The second condition for an effective error-correction mechanism is that the expert organisation operates in a social context fostering the sustained generation of varied criticism. The social context of central banks refers to their internal organisation, but it also includes the broader community of specialists and non-specialists on topics related to central banking such as monetary policy and financial regulation. In this section, we will see that the current social context has a potential for sustained criticism generation, especially because the research community on central banking is vibrant. But there is something highly worrisome about this context: the centrality of central banks themselves. Since they control much of the material resources and symbolic capital, we have reasons to suspect that research is skewed and that some types of criticism are muted in comparison to an alternative social context where testimonial expertise on central banking would be more broadly shared.

In recent decades, central banks have been through a process of 'scientization',[16] with impressive results: employing large research staff, cultivating links with university researchers, organising workshops, producing peer-reviewed publications and publishing massively in academic journals. The Fed has been a pioneer in this domain (see the table below for the number of its staff economists since the 1990s). The Reserve's board has an army of 392 PhD economists and the twelve regional banks have 416 more. Already in 2003, when the total was not 808 but 495 economists, Lawrence H. White estimated that 'the Fed employ[ed] full-time about 27 per cent more macro/money/banking economists than the top 50 US academic economics departments put together'.[17] These numbers do not even count the numerous researchers coming as visiting scholars to one of the Fed institutions in any given year, nor the economists who are paid as consultants on a project.[18]

Number of staff economists in the Federal Reserve System since 1993[19]

	1993	2003	2017
Board of Governors	189	220	392
Regional Banks	171	275	416
Total	360	495	808
Average annual growth rate:	3.2% (1993–2003)		3.6% (2003–17)

The other major central banks are on a similar path. The ECB strives 'to establish intellectual leadership within the world-wide central bank-related research community',[20] and the Bank of England pledges 'to cultivate an extensive research community that spans the Bank and beyond'.[21] The global result of all these efforts to further research is that the dominance of central banks inside the research community has steadily grown. One indicator of this increasing dominance is the share of articles in the main peer-reviewed journals that are signed by at least one author affiliated with a central bank (see Figure 3). Thirty years ago, less than one in five articles included an author employed by a central bank, in 2015 the proportion was slightly more

Central Banking Expertise

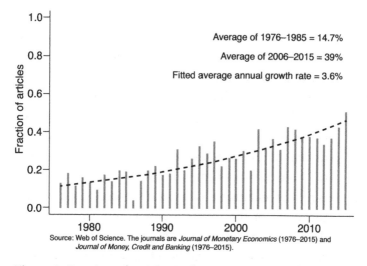

Source: Web of Science. The journals are *Journal of Monetary Economics* (1976–2015) and *Journal of Money, Credit and Banking* (1976–2015).

Figure 3 Fraction of articles in the two main specialised academic journals with at least one author working at a central bank

than half. And this does not even include researchers with close connections to central banks although they have another primary affiliation (e.g., visiting scholars, consultants).

Why does it matter that central banks are the dominant institutions in the research community on central banking? We first want to grant that the *integration* of central banks into the research community has evident positive consequences, before turning to why we should worry about their *dominant* position.

Do Central Banks Serve the People?

There are three reasons why the fact that central banks participate in research is something to be welcomed. First, we want some of the topics that are actively researched to be aligned with the needs of practitioners. The economic world is in constant flux. As *regulatory* experts, it is in the interest of central bankers to have a steady flow of research that is directly relevant to their day-to-day work. One way to make research topics match the regulators' needs is to let regulators allocate a fraction of the financial resources of the research community to what they deem to be priorities. Second, for research critical of some of the consensual beliefs of central bankers to reliably reach their ears – and thus have at least the potential to correct their errors – channels of communication need to be open. Establishing vibrant research divisions inside central banks which are connected on one side to the regulatory experts and, on the other, to the external research community is one way to establish these necessary communication channels. Third, the regulatory experts often have data and practical knowledge that can inform further research. Central banks indeed have a privileged access to detailed monetary, financial and economic data, which can be extremely useful to researchers. Beyond data, central banks may also provide insights into theory because, as Mark

Carney puts it, 'the practice of central banking has frequently moved ahead of the theory of central banking'.[22]

Given these three reasons, central banks need to be integrated into a research community to properly serve the people. But, again, criticism generation is hampered when central banks become dominant. It is hampered in terms of both its amount and its variety.

On the amount of criticism

With respect to the amount or intensity of criticism, the incentive structure is different for researchers working for central banks than it is for researchers who have a different primary affiliation, but the dominant position of central banks has worrisome effects in both cases.

For researchers working for central banks, there is the possibility of direct censure. The ECB emphasises on its website: 'All our research products have an editorial board that ensures the research is of high quality.'[23] What does it mean to be of high quality? In a 2015 anonymous interview, a senior ECB manager asserted: '[W]ould we publish a paper that is contrary to the ECB policy? I don't think so

. . . Sometimes you read the ECB WP series and you already know the conclusion.'[24] Even though cases of actual censure are hard to document and might in fact be scarce, the possibility of being identified as an internal black sheep is likely to act as a deterrent. Standard strategic considerations involving career advancement and general work climate should lead us to expect that research staff will rarely advance radical criticism.

For economic researchers working at another institution, the incentives created by the dominance of central banks are different, but nonetheless pre-occupying. Having your work recognised by central banks through fellowships, contracts and workshop invitations has become a crucial marker of expertise. And there is evidence that voicing strong criticism can lead to being side-lined by central banks – for instance, Paul Krugman, although famous, suffered a ten-year exclusion from the Jackson Hole meeting (the great annual gathering of central bankers) after he criticised the Fed's policies under Alan Greenspan.[25]

Furthermore, now that central banks are dominant in knowledge production, their senior staff and close collaborators have also become numerous among the gate-keepers of the specialised conversation, probably often outnumbering independent scholars. For example, among the thirty-three editorial board members of the *Journal of Monetary Economics* in August 2017, only eight had never been on the payroll of a central bank (although they had all 'visited' one) while sixteen were still employed by a central bank (mostly the Fed).[26] Although we have scant data on the profile of *referees* for academic journals in the field, we should also expect that a significant proportion of them are closely tied to central banks.

The structural result is that, although participants in the specialised conversation might not even realise it,[27] sympathisers of the incumbent institutions have many ways to mute criticism. We must emphasise that there is no need for a coordinated strategy to reach this result: the combined force of professional socialisation, selection effects and personal bonds is enough to render the current dominance of central banks in knowledge production unhealthy.

On the diversity of criticism

With respect to the issue of the diversity of criticism, we can distinguish between an effect on the diversity of subjects and a broader effect on the diversity of perspectives.

Do Central Banks Serve the People?

Although regulatory experts have a legitimate interest in directing part of research towards their needs, this influence becomes detrimental if the proportion of such research is extremely large. Regulators have an understandable preference for research that informs their *current* concerns. Consequently, research that asks more fundamental questions about the possible futures of central banking is unlikely to be favoured in funding allocation or to be rewarded with symbolic capital. For instance, one might naively expect that research on the *justification* for the current level of independence enjoyed by central banks would be thriving today. Since what central banks do has changed quite substantially since the 2007–8 financial crisis, reconsidering the old arguments for independence seems necessary. But this topic is, in fact, extremely peripheral in the research produced by central banks: out of the more than 9,500 research papers produced by central banks worldwide between 2008 and July 2017, only five addressed this issue.[28]

Another concern with respect to the diversity of criticism stems from the low diversity of the members of the community. As indicated above, there are solid reasons to believe that a community with members from diverse backgrounds will be able to generate more diverse lines of criticism. For cen-

94

tral banks, uniformity is most striking at the level of governing bodies; for instance, the Governing Council of the ECB has only two women among its twenty-five members.

Beyond questions of gender, which is only one dimension of diversity, there is also an issue with professional and theoretical backgrounds. Central bankers who are charged with regulating the banking and financial sector have often worked for major firms in this sector.[29] Furthermore, they get much of their non-academic, external advice from this sector. For instance, a recent report has revealed that the ECB's twenty-two advisory groups include almost only representatives from private financial institutions: they hold 508 of the 517 seats in these groups.[30] Uniformity is also a characteristic of the theoretical background of the central banking staff: today, both researchers and decision makers are overwhelmingly trained in mainstream economics (a notable exception being Jerome Powell, Donald Trump's pick for the top job at the Fed from February 2018). This uniformity of perspective is a significant reason for the myopia of the central banking community in the years leading to the great financial crisis.[31] Unfortunately, the trend does not seem to have moved towards more professional and theoretical diversity since then.

Do Central Banks Serve the People?

Finally, ethnic diversity in central banks has also become an issue recently: the 'Fed Up' movement in the United States claims that the Fed fails to do research on the negative effects of monetary policies on specific ethnic groups. It asks both for a more diverse board and for a Fed research programme dedicated to these issues.[32] In general, the composition of central banks today is too homogeneous for their dominance not to have a detrimental effect on the diversity of criticism towards themselves.

In sum, the dominant position of central banks in the contemporary research community on central banking might be justifiable from the perspective of regulatory expertise: central bankers want to have strong research teams so they can make well-informed decisions. But this dominant position exhibits a great number of symptoms associated with criticism hindrance. In 1993, Milton Friedman already advanced the following diagnosis for the Fed: he 'saw few among the academic community who were prepared to criticize the Fed policy'.[33] Because the dominance of central banks globally has only increased since then, his diagnosis is even more compelling today.

Central bankers and dissent uptake

The last condition for an effective error-correction mechanism is that testimonial experts have the proper dispositions to adjust their beliefs when faced with relevant criticism.

Prominent central bankers, including Alan Greenspan, have publicly changed their mind on important issues. For instance, most central bankers now maintain that macroprudential supervision is crucial because, contrary to earlier beliefs, the banking system suffers from unstable dynamics that could lead to an economic collapse if left unsupervised. In this case, it seems that economic calamity was necessary for central bankers to change their mind.

But we have reason to be more hopeful for the future. Central bankers face strong incentives, as *regulatory* experts, to fulfil their mandate of price and financial stability. If there is solid evidence that some of their beliefs and modes of action are not conducive to serving these goals, their own professional survival is threatened. In these cases, personal interests align with a concern for truth, which makes belief revision more likely (although not automatic, as recent history teaches us).

Are there also cases where there is instead a

misalignment between truth-seeking and personal interests? There are indeed. First, there is a tension between asking fundamental questions about the possible futures of central banking and the short-term regulatory interest of protecting the reputation of central banks especially vis-à-vis financial market participants: if central bankers appear undecided, expectations on financial markets may run wild. We can thus expect that central bankers will change their mind on crucial issues only when their regulatory goals are strongly threatened, as was the case in the aftermath of the 2007–8 financial crisis. Second, in a context where senior central bankers will often continue their careers in the private financial sector once their mandate is over, they are less likely to argue for turning back the clock on financialisation. Third, members of the central banking community benefit from the current political arrangement where they enjoy considerable independence from the state and have, since the crisis, increased their regulatory influence. Instead of being neutral information providers, their partiality in favour of independence may at times conflict with the institutional arrangement that would best serve the people.

Conclusion

We need *testimonial* experts in a complex and uncertain world. Today, central bankers are the main trusted source of information on monetary policy and financial regulation. Yet, this chapter has spelled out reasons why the testimonial expertise of central bankers does not optimally serve the people. The heart of the problem is that the interests of central banks in controlling the monetary system – that is, in succeeding as *regulatory* experts – get in the way of their performance as detached and impartial testimonial experts. This tension is especially serious when we need advice on the potential alternative futures of central banking. On this topic, we have strong reasons to believe that today's central banks do not represent credible information providers.

5

Whither Central Banking? Institutional Options for the Future

The challenges presented in the previous chapters make one doubt whether today's central banks are serving the people as well as they could. Can we think of different institutional arrangements that would allow our polities to achieve their objectives, including but not limited to price stability and financial stability, in a more effective way? We believe the answer to this question is yes.

Many observers of central banking agree that the practice is bound to change in the years to come, indeed that this process of change has already begun. As early after the start of the financial crisis as 2010, for example, Charles Goodhart pondered 'the changing role of central banks', highlighting that the certainties of the CBI era are gone and that central banking will be forced to adapt.[1] The arguments of this book have lent further support to the position that a return to the CBI template is not desirable. One of the important lessons of the 2007 financial crisis is that central banks should not be blind to financial instability and distributive concerns.

Moving forward into this new era of central banking, our main goal lies in encouraging all of us to take seriously the three challenges we have set out in this book. In this last chapter, we shall discuss some of the possible institutional responses to these challenges.

We have chosen to divide the reform proposals in question into two basic categories. We shall first present, with respect to the three challenges we have identified, a menu of immediate reforms that would represent a step in the right direction. While controversial, the reform proposals in this category do not stray very far from the status quo in the sense that, by and large, they preserve the way central banking works today. In a second step, we will turn to some more fundamental reforms. The latter require radically rethinking aspects of the financial arrangements of our society. By their fundamental nature, they also turn out to be even more controversial. Our goal here is not to defend them, but to encourage everyone to take them seriously. Our discussion does not have the ambition to be comprehensive.

One idea that we do not include is doing away with central banks altogether.

Immediate reforms

Inequalities and integration of policy objectives: In relation to containing the inegalitarian side effects of unconventional monetary policy, Chapter 2 distinguished two basic models. The first is to preserve the current, narrow mandate of central banks, but put in place channels of communication and coordination between them and other government agencies; the second consists in widening their mandate and asking central banks themselves to actively pursue a wider set of policy objectives, such as for instance limiting inequalities. Let us now look at these two models in some more detail.

What would an increased level of communication between government agencies look like under the first model? Regarding the crucial communication between monetary and fiscal authorities, for instance, one can imagine a joint committee composed of members of the central bank and the treasury. The task of this committee would be to document the ways in which different policy instruments in one area impact, and potentially undermine, the pursuit of policy objectives in the other. In addition, the committee would be charged with coming up with recommendations for how best to react to these side effects, and how to address the resulting trade-offs.

Turning to the second model, what does it mean to make the mandate of central banks 'sensitive' to distributive concerns without it becoming a fundamental reform? First, it means more than a mere tie-breaker criterion, where central banks should choose the less inegalitarian policy from two policies that score equally well in terms of price stability; in fact, this tie breaking is something their mandate requires them to do already. Second, it means less than adding a permanent objective of curbing inequality to the mandate of central banks, which would be radical indeed. Third, and this is the middle path we favour, central banks could be required to factor in distributive concerns in specific circumstances, namely when they consider using extraordinary instruments. The expected impact on a central bank's balance sheet could be a way to distinguish extraordinary from benign instruments. For instance, launching a QE programme dramatically increases the assets held by a central bank. Decision makers should thus take distributive considerations into account before setting out their policy.[2]

How can this be put into practice while balancing effective policy making with democratic accountability? On the one hand, central banks could be given *prior* instructions on how to address policy trade-offs, for instance by imposing a specific composition of types of financial assets that will have to be bought in future rounds of quantitative easing; on the other hand, it could mean more stringent accountability mechanisms where, *after the fact*, central bankers will have to report on, and justify, the ways in which monetary policy impacts other policy objectives, including the distribution of income and wealth.

In Chapter 2, we also scrutinised the inegalitarian effects of corporate bond buying schemes. Once the inevitable bias of such schemes is acknowledged, one might as well channel this bias in a desirable direction. At a minimum, central banks should respect ethical guidelines in their purchases, as most institutional investors do. For example, an ethical council screens the investments of the Norwegian Oil Fund. Central banks could also play a more active role in supporting non-monetary social objectives. Civil society activists today call for Strategic and Green QE: the central bank would finance *private* strategically important or green infrastructure projects selected by fiscal authorities or other agencies, such as the European Investment Bank (EIB).[3] The central banks of Japan and South Korea, for instance, promote specific sectors with their purchases, including childcare services and corporations whose mission includes environmental protection.[4]

Alternatively, as Mark Blyth and Eric Lonergan have suggested for the European context, the ECB could buy bonds from the European Investment Bank, which in turn directs programmes aimed at supporting growth and reducing inequalities.[5] Today, central bankers tend to shy away from such programmes, because they fear that their explicitly political character and the need for more coordination with other agencies threaten their independence. However, if one accepts that central banks are already up to their neck in political waters, taking this next step should not be taboo.

Financial dominance: When the financial crisis struck, some people anticipated that the financial deregulation that had marked the era of the great moderation would be reversed. However, this did not happen. While new measures have been introduced (such as stress tests and slightly higher capital requirements), they do not decisively address the roots of the financial crisis. The problematic model of market-based banking continues to be dominant in Europe, the leverage of financial institutions is still too high, and remuneration levels in the financial industry remain disconnected from average wages.

Financial authorities need to introduce pieces of regulation that reduce the financialisation of our economies. The kind of regulations we have in mind here are far from revolutionary and are often grouped together under the label of macro-prudential regulation. Such measures include, but are not limited to, raising the reserve requirements for commercial banks at the central bank, separating commercial banking from investment banking, regulating the shadow-banking sector, tightening the collateral frameworks for the interbank lending market as well as for central bank reserves, a better alignment of financial sector bonuses with long-term performance, banning or restricting the use of certain kinds of financial activities or instruments (e.g. proprietary trading by banks or short-selling), introducing a financial transaction tax.

Such macroprudential measures not only promote financial stability, they also enhance the transmission of monetary policy to the real economy, by curbing the speculative use of central bank liquidity. The fact that central banks have not pushed harder for macroprudential reforms corroborates the hypothesis of financial dominance. It is a symptom of the latter and of the resulting short-sightedness of the ECB that it actually *opposes* a financial transaction tax, suggesting that it would undermine the liquidity of markets important to its open-market operations (see Chapter 3).

Central bank expertise: Chapter 4 has demonstrated both the homogeneity of central bank decision makers and the concentration of scientific research on monetary policy under the auspices of central banks. Both of these characteristics are unhealthy from the perspective of the role of central bankers as testimonial experts. Two reform proposals aim to address these pitfalls.

First, the dominance of central banks in the scientific community on monetary policy and other money-related issues needs to be reduced. Several instruments are available to pursue this goal: funding for academic projects on monetary policy outside central banks can be topped up; high-quality publication outlets should be open to a diversity of theoretical positions, which could be partly achieved by diversifying their editorial boards.

Second, the current lack of diversity in central bank decision-making bodies undermines their capacity to serve the people. With Janet Yellen of the

Do Central Banks Serve the People?

Federal Reserve being one notable exception, central bankers in western economies tend to be older white men, trained in mainstream economics, and with a background in the financial sector. Homogeneity reduces the capacity for error-correction in the beliefs of central bankers. More women, more intellectual and ethnic diversity, the representation of people from less privileged socioeconomic backgrounds, fewer central bankers who get shot into a seat on the board through the revolving door between central banks and the financial sector – all of these can be defended not necessarily on grounds of making central banks more representative, but because we have reasons to believe it would lead them to be better experts. Activists such as those in the Fed Up movement are right to campaign on these issues.[6]

Fundamental reforms

We believe that the more thoroughgoing reforms we are about to discuss are, at least at first sight, attractive because they address the challenges discussed in previous chapters. Whether they are desirable *all things considered* as well as feasible can only be determined by more thorough research and debates. Given the importance of the challenges central banking faces today, thinking merely inside the box is no longer an option.

Inequalities and integration of policy objectives: The negative distributive consequences of unconventional monetary policies since the financial crisis are partly due to the fact that central banks have had to inject huge amounts of liquidity in order to obtain the desired outcome in terms of price or output stimulation.

One way to remedy this situation is to cut out the middlemen. Under today's institutional set-up, central banks have to rely on commercial banks to pass on the extra liquidity to consumers and investors in order to produce the desired effects on prices and output. If commercial banks are reluctant to do so, why not give the money directly to consumers and investors? This is the idea behind the so-called *helicopter drop* first put forward by Milton Friedman.[7] The amount of liquidity that would need to be injected compared to the indirect method of QE would be considerably lower, and the inegalitarian consequences could be avoided. Critics fear that helicopter drops would prove inflationary. However, two responses are available to this concern. First, if a helicopter drop leads to inflation, this merely shows that too much money was injected; this inflation can be controlled through conventional contractionary monetary policy. Second, it is worth noting that QE faces its own challenges. Even though the Fed has started in 2017 to 'unwind' its balance sheet, we thus far lack a good demonstration of how the exit from QE actually works.

Note that for the purposes of our argument, we do not need to establish that a helicopter drop is a policy without shortcomings. The possibility that the benefits of reduced inegalitarian consequences *outweigh* the eventual shortcomings of a helicopter drop is enough to put the latter on the agenda.

A similarly controversial policy with the potential of avoiding collateral distributive damage is the monetising of public debt, that is, financing public expenditure or repaying public debt through central bank money creation. Long considered a taboo in monetary policy circles, it has been put back on the agenda, notably by Adair Turner's book *Between Debt and the Devil*. Turner makes a plausible case that the dangers of monetising public debt are the lesser evil compared to fighting a crisis-induced debt overhang through austerity.

Financial dominance: The first victim of the power of financial markets is financial stability. When private financial institutions become systemically important, this leads to central banks making compromises when it comes to ensuring financial stability, and the toleration of unsustainable levels of leverage in the banking sector.

One sure way to address the problem of leverage in the financial sector is to strip commercial banks of the capacity to create money in the form of debt deposits. Two fundamental reforms have the potential to address this issue: the shift to 100 per cent reserve banking and the introduction of central bank digital currencies. Promoted by the British Currency School in the nineteenth century and by Irving Fisher in the 1930s, the 100 per cent reserve banking proposal reduces the role of commercial banks to that of intermediaries.[8] They would no longer have the capacity to create deposits, but would have to rely on someone saving money and asking them to invest it before they can make a loan. As for the saver, she can choose to either hold risk-free money in the form of 100 per cent deposits or invest her capital while accepting that its value might diminish.

The advantage of 100 per cent reserve banking is that it significantly enhances financial stability. For instance, the danger of bank runs during economic downturns is virtually eliminated. Critics fear that shifting to a 100 per cent reserve system would necessarily have a negative impact on economic growth. We cannot assess this empirical question here, but it is worth pointing out that as long as the reduced leverage comes from a reduction in investment in existing assets such as houses or stocks, this is not a foregone conclusion. That being said, it seems plausible to think that a reform towards 100 per cent reserve banking would have to be introduced gradually.

Another way to make the use of central bank liquidity more effective and avoid financial dominance would be to allow citizens to open accounts at the central bank. Until now, technical issues have complicated the opening of citizens' accounts at central banks: managing customer contacts and the record keeping of customer transactions were deemed overwhelming. Yet, the emergence of digital currencies, such as bitcoin, opens up new possibilities. With the use of blockchain technology, citizens and businesses could open central bank digital accounts and engage in bilateral transactions directly overseen by the central bank. The concentration of citizens' deposits in the central bank would also ease the transition to 100 per cent reserve banking and widen the range of options for monetary policy. For example, it would facilitate 'helicopter drops' into citizens' accounts in order to boost aggregate demand. The direct manipulation of customer balances could also help central bankers to fine-tune their monetary policy towards certain geographical areas or lower income deciles.

However, tightening the relationship between citizens and central banks might also have downsides. The centralisation of payment systems and information about citizens' accounts would transform the central bank into a modern Leviathan. Would central banks be allowed to grant loans? Would they be in competition with other financial institutions to acquire new customers? Beyond the issue of power concentration, current central bank research on the prospect of digital currencies highlights serious feasibility and security concerns.

Central bank expertise: One of the proposals to encourage research diversity discussed under 'immediate reforms' suggested reducing the dominance of central banks in producing research on monetary policy. This is easier said than done, precisely because central banks in their role as regulatory experts have incentives to dominate this research agenda.

A more radical idea that promises to be more effective is to try to isolate the research activities of central banks from their policy agenda. This goal could be achieved by converting the research units of central banks into entities that operate at arm's length from the policy-setting units. Imagine the ECB having to set aside part of its budget for research, with the allocation of these funds decided by a decision-making body that is independent from the ECB's monetary policy committee. Of course, the latter could still request certain types of research to be conducted, but it would no longer have full control of the research agenda. This independent research unit could have an ambitious public outreach programme leading its members to regularly intervene in the media and at various public events, something that today's communication-conscious central bankers are reluctant to do. Such a division of labour within central banks would allow them to reconcile their two roles of testimonial as well as regulatory experts.

Conclusion

We have made the case in the foregoing chapters that central banking today, and since the financial crisis in particular, faces three important challenges. First, the unconventional instruments such as QE that central banks have used since the crisis have unintended negative consequences; more specifically, they exacerbate already substantial inequalities in income and wealth. Second, while the literature on monetary policy has focused on independence from governments, the operation of monetary policy under financial dominance has gone largely unnoticed; the leverage financial markets have over central banks is deeply problematic. Third and finally, there is a conflict between two facets of the expertise that we ask of central bankers; the way things are set up today, when they do a good job at being regulatory experts, this leads to a concentration of scientific expertise that undermines their role as testimonial experts.

In this chapter, we have indicated a series of potential reforms to address these challenges. All of these reforms can be implemented even in the absence of an immediate crisis. But it is well known that crises offer unique windows of opportunity to implement significant reforms. As Milton Friedman put it: 'Only a crisis – actual or perceived – produces real change. When that crisis occurs, the actions that are taken depend on the ideas that are lying around. That, I believe, is our basic function: to develop alternatives to existing policies, to keep them alive and available until the politically impossible becomes the politically inevitable.'[9] The success of Friedman's political agenda after the collapse of the Bretton Woods system is a case in point.

No blueprint for significant reforms was lying around when the 2007 financial crisis struck. As a result, and compounded by the protection of powerful interests, the crisis did not significantly weaken prevailing economic ideas or the leverage of financial institutions over political authorities.[10]

Since another major financial crisis is bound to happen, we should be better prepared next time to address two disconcerting trends of modern economies: rising socioeconomic inequalities and increasing financialisation. The deterrent effect of a blueprint for significant reforms on the risky behaviour of financial actors might even help postpone the next crisis. Most importantly, we must make sure that the next financial crisis is a real game changer and realigns the activities of central banks with the interests of the people.

Notes

Introduction: Central Banks Ought to Serve the People

1 Board of Governors of the Federal Reserve System, 'Careers at the Federal Reserve Board', www.feder alreserve.gov/careers/files/brochure.pdf.
2 Mark Carney, 'One Mission. One Bank. Promoting the Good of the People of the United Kingdom', speech at City University London, 18 March 2014, 3, www.bis.org/review/r140319b.pdf.
3 Ibid., 5.
4 Christian Noyer, 'Central Banking: The Way Forward?', opening speech to the International Symposium of the Banque de France, 7 November 2014, www.bis.org/review/r141110c.htm.
5 Center for Macroeconomics Surveys, 'The Future of Central Bank Independence', 20 December 2016, http://cfmsurvey.org/surveys/future-central-bank-ind ependence.

Chapter 1 Central Banking: The Essentials

1 The diffusion of the CBI template was propelled by the spread of neoliberal beliefs amongst policy makers, geopolitical changes (such as the collapse of the communist bloc), and pressures from international organisations (such as the EU and the IMF). See Kathleen McNamara, 'Rational Fictions: Central Bank Independence and the Social Logic of Delegation', *West European Politics* 25, no. 1 (2002): 47–76; Juliet Johnson, *Priests of Prosperity: How Central Bankers Transformed the Postcommunist World* (Ithaca: Cornell University Press, 2016).

2 Charles Goodhart and Ellen Meade, 'Central Banks and Supreme Courts', *Moneda y Crédito* 218 (2004): 11–42.

3 John Rawls, *Justice as Fairness: A Restatement* (Cambridge, MA: Belknap Press of Harvard University Press, 2001), 8–9.

4 Alan S. Blinder et al., 'Necessity as the Mother of Invention: Monetary Policy After the Crisis', *Economic Policy* 32, no. 92 (2017) 707–55.

5 In the last few years, the value of assets held by the Bank of Japan has grown at annual rates of roughly 25%. In early September 2017, assets held represented 92% of annual GDP, far above most other central banks (data retrieved from FRED, Federal Reserve Bank of St. Louis, 8 September 2017).

6 Jagjit S. Chadha, Luisa Corrado and Jack Meaning, 'Reserves, Liquidity and Money: An Assessment of Balance Sheet Policies', *BIS Paper*, no. 66 (2012).

7 Clément Fontan, 'Frankenstein in Europe: The Impact of the European Central Bank on the Management of the Eurozone Crisis', *Politique européenne* 42, no. 4 (2013): 22–45.

8 This fact is largely recognised by central bank governors. See Blinder et al., 'Necessity as the Mother of Invention', secs. 2–3.

9 Charles Goodhart et al., eds., *Central Banking at a Crossroads: Europe and Beyond* (London: Anthem Press, 2014).

10 Group of Thirty, ed., *Fundamentals of Central Banking: Lessons from the Crisis* (Washington, DC: Group of Thirty, 2015).

Chapter 2 Central Banking and Inequalities

1 Mark Carney, 'Inclusive Capitalism: Creating a Sense of the Systemic', 27 May 2014, www.bis.org/review/r140528b.htm. See also the important report by the Bank of England: 'The Distributional Effects of Asset Purchases', London: Bank of England, 12 July 2012, www.bankofengland.co.uk/-/media/boe/files/news/2012/july/the-distributional-effects-of-ass et-purchases-paper.

2 Benoît Coeuré, 'The Economic Consequences of Low Interest Rates', European Central Bank, 9 October 2013, www.ecb.europa.eu/press/key/date/2013/ht ml/sp131009.en.html.

3 For a more comprehensive treatment of this question, see Peter Dietsch, 'Normative Dimensions of Central Banking: How the Guardians of Financial

Markets Affect Justice', in *Just Financial Markets: Finance in a Just Society*, ed. Lisa Herzog (Oxford: Oxford University Press, 2017), 231–49. For a perspective from contemporary monetary theory, see Michael Woodford, *Interest and Prices: Foundations of a Theory of Monetary Policy* (Princeton: Princeton University Press, 2011).

4 Clément Fontan, François Claveau and Peter Dietsch, 'Central Banking and Inequalities: Taking off the Blinders', *Politics, Philosophy & Economics* 15, no. 4 (2016): 319–57.

5 John Rawls, *A Theory of Justice: Revised Edition* (Cambridge, MA: Belknap Press of Harvard University Press, 1999).

6 David Miles, 'Asset Prices, Saving and the Wider Effects of Monetary Policy', 1 March 2012, www. bankofengland.co.uk/-/media/boe/files/news/2012/ march/asset-prices-saving-and-the-wider-effects-of-monetary-policy-speech-by-david-miles.

7 Another effect is the policy signalling effect: with central banks including long-term debt into their purchases, they are signalling to markets that interest rates will stay low for the foreseeable future. See Bank of England, 'The Distributional Effects of Asset Purchases'; Olivier Coibion et al., 'Innocent Bystanders? Monetary Policy and Inequality in the U.S.', NBER Working Paper 18170, Cambridge, MA, 2012, provide a good overview of the various transmission channels of monetary policy.

8 Michael McLeay, Amar Radia and Ryland Thomas, 'Money Creation in the Modern Economy', *Bank of*

England, Quarterly Bulletin (2014): 24. This publication by three employees of the Bank of England provides an excellent introduction to the way money is created in today's economy.

9 Adair Turner, *Between Debt and the Devil: Money, Credit, and Fixing Global Finance* (Princeton: Princeton University Press, 2014) highlights the importance of this question.

10 See Emmanuel Saez, 'Striking it Richer: The Evolution of Top Incomes in the United States (Updated with 2015 Preliminary Estimates)', 2, https://eml.berkeley.edu/~saez/saez-UStopincomes-2015.pdf. For studies on the impact of QE, specifically on inequalities, see for instance Jakob de Haan and Sylvester Eijffinger, 'The Politics of Central Bank Independence', DNB Working Paper, no. 539, De Nederlandsche Bank, December 2016; William R. White, 'Ultra Easy Monetary Policy and the Law of Unintended Consequences', Federal Reserve Bank of Dallas, 21 August 2012, www.dallasfed.org/assets/documents/institute/wpapers/2012/0126.pdf; Bank of England, 'The Distributional Effects of Asset Purchases'; European Central Bank, 'Annual Report 2016', 2016, 48–51, www.ecb.europa.eu/pub/pdf/annrep/ar2016en.pdf.

11 Ben Bernanke, the former Chair of the Federal Reserve, for instance, cites several countervailing factors that lead him to question the extent to which monetary policy has contributed to rising inequalities in recent years. Specifically, he mentions job creation, benefits to the middle class, the relative merits

of 2% inflation compared to deflation for debtors, and the idea that Fed policy merely returned stock markets to trend rather than boosted them. See Ben S. Bernanke, 'Monetary Policy and Inequality', *Brookings Institution*, 1 June 2015. While these factors no doubt play a role, it is implausible to think that they are as important as the inequality-driving asset price boom itself.

12 See our in-depth discussion of the TINA argument in Fontan, Claveau and Dietsch, 'Central Banking and Inequalities'.

13 We shall come back to this issue in Chapter 5.

14 'ECB-fuelled Market Smooths Path for Volkswagen's Return', Reuters, 15 April 2016.

15 Sini Matikainen, Emanuele Campiglio and Dimitri Zenghelis, 'Policy Brief: The Climate Impact of Quantitative Easing', Grantham Research Institute, 2017.

16 Some monetary policy theorists explicitly recognise the need for more integration of policy objectives. See for example Markus K. Brunnermeier and Yuliy Sannikov, 'Redistributive Monetary Policy', in *Jackson Hole Symposium*, vol. 1 (Federal Reserve Bank of Kansas City, KS, 2012), 331–84; Charles Goodhart, 'The Changing Role of Central Banks', BIS Working Paper, no. 326 (2010).

17 For a representative expression of this view, see James M. Buchanan and Richard E. Wagner, *Democracy in Deficit: The Political Legacy of Lord Keynes* (Indianapolis: Liberty Fund, 1977).

18 European Parliament, 'Report on the Enquiry

on the Role and Operations of the Troika (ECB, Commission and IMF) with Regard to the Euro Area Programme Countries – A7-0149/2014', 28 February 2014, www.europarl.europa.eu/sides/get Doc.do?pubRef=-//EP//TEXT+REPORT+A7-2014-01 49+0+DOC+XML+V0//EN.

19 See for instance William Bernhard, J. Lawrence Broz and William Roberts Clark, 'The Political Economy of Monetary Institutions', *International Organization* 56, no. 4 (September 2002).

20 The locus classicus of this argument in the literature is Finn E. Kydland and Edward C. Prescott, 'Rules Rather than Discretion: The Inconsistency of Optimal Plans', *Journal of Political Economy* 85, no. 3 (1 June 1977): 473–91; Robert J. Barro and David B. Gordon, 'A Positive Theory of Monetary Policy in a Natural Rate Model', *Journal of Political Economy* 91, no. 4 (1 August 1983): 589–610, develop this argument further. For insightful critical discussions of time inconsistency, see James Forder, 'Central Bank Independence – Conceptual Clarifications and Interim Assessment', *Oxford Economic Papers* 50, no. 3 (1 July 1998): 307–34; and Charles Goodhart, 'Game Theory for Central Bankers: A Report to the Governor of the Bank of England', *Journal of Economic Literature* (1994): 101–14. For a philo-sophical perspective, see Jon Elster, 'Constitutional Courts and Central Banks: Suicide Prevention or Suicide Pact?', *East European Constitutional Review* 3, nos. 3 & 4 (1994): 66–71.

21 The Taylor rule makes nominal interest rates

responsive to two measures: the difference between actual inflation and target inflation as well as the difference between GDP and potential GDP.

22 Waldyr Dutra Areosa and Marta B.M. Areosa, 'The Inequality Channel of Monetary Transmission', *Journal of Macroeconomics* 48 (2016): 214–30.

23 Otmar Issing et al., *Monetary Policy in the Euro Area: Strategy and Decision-Making at the European Central Bank* (Cambridge: Cambridge University Press, 2001); see also Bennett T. McCallum, 'Crucial Issues Concerning Central Bank Independence', *Journal of Monetary Economics*, Rules and Discretion in Monetary Policy, 39, no. 1 (1 June 1997): 99–112.

24 Alan S. Blinder, 'Distinguished Lecture on Economics in Government: What Central Bankers Could Learn from Academics – and Vice Versa', *The Journal of Economic Perspectives* 11, no. 2 (1997): 14.

25 Kenneth S. Rogoff, 'The Optimal Degree of Commitment to an Intermediate Monetary Target', *The Quarterly Journal of Economics* 100, no. 4 (1985): 1169; Forder observes that 'Rogoff's argument has undoubtedly become the hub of the central bank independence literature.' Forder, 'Central Bank Independence', 313.

26 Forder, 'Central Bank Independence', 327.

27 Issing et al., *Monetary Policy in the Euro Area*, 36.

28 Alberto Alesina and Lawrence H. Summers, 'Central Bank Independence and Macroeconomic Performance: Some Comparative Evidence', *Journal*

of Money, Credit and Banking 25, no. 2 (1993): 151–62.

Chapter 3 Central Banking and Finance

1 Kenneth Dyson, 'The Age of the Euro: A Structural Break? Europeanization, Convergence, and Power in Central Banking', in *Central Banks in the Age of the Euro: Europeanization, Convergence, and Power*, ed. Kenneth H. F. Dyson and Martin Marcussen (Oxford: Oxford University Press, 2009), 10; and Fontan, 'Frankenstein in Europe'.

2 Ismail Erturk, *Financialization At Work: Key Texts and Commentary* (London and New York: Routledge, 2008); Gerald A. Epstein, ed., *Financialization and the World Economy* (Cheltenham: Edward Elgar Publishing, 2005).

3 Colin Crouch, *The Strange Non-Death of Neo-Liberalism* (Cambridge: Polity, 2011); Ewald Engelen, *After the Great Complacence: Financial Crisis and the Politics of Reform* (Oxford: Oxford University Press, 2011).

4 See Iain Hardie and David Howarth, *Market-Based Banking and the International Financial Crisis* (Oxford: Oxford University Press, 2013).

5 Daniela Gabor and Cornel Ban, 'Banking on Bonds: The New Links Between States and Markets', *Journal of Common Market Studies* 54, no. 3 (2016): 623.

6 Charles P. Kindleberger and Robert Z. Aliber, *Manias, Panics, and Crashes: A History of Financial Crises* (Hoboken: John Wiley & Sons, 2005).

7 Carmen M. Reinhart and Kenneth S. Rogoff, *This Time Is Different: Eight Centuries of Financial Folly* (Princeton: Princeton University Press, 2009).

8 Ben Bernanke, 'Housing, Housing Finance, and Monetary Policy', Federal Reserve, 31 August 2007.

9 Anat Admati and Martin Hellwig, *The Bankers' New Clothes: What's Wrong with Banking and What to Do About It* (Princeton: Princeton University Press, 2014); and Turner, *Between Debt and the Devil*.

10 US House of Representatives, 'The Financial Crisis and the Role of Federal Regulators: Hearing Before the Committee on Oversight and Government Reform' (2008), www.gpo.gov/fdsys/pkg/CHRG-110hhrg55764/html/CHRG-110hhrg55764.htm.

11 Alan Greenspan, 'Economic Flexibility', Federal Reserve, 27 September 2005.

12 Greta R. Krippner, *Capitalizing on Crisis* (Cambridge, MA: Harvard University Press, 2011).

13 Marcus Miller, Paul Weller and Lei Zhang, 'Moral Hazard and the US Stock Market: Analysing the "Greenspan Put"', *The Economic Journal* 112, no. 478 (1 March 2002): C171–86.

14 Gabor and Ban, 'Banking on Bonds'.

15 In the academic literature, financial dominance depicts the inability of central bankers to control moral hazard risks when bailing out the financial system. See Brunnermeier and Sannikov, 'Redistributive Monetary Policy', and Hervé Hannoun, 'Monetary Policy in the Crisis: Testing the Limits of Monetary Policy', speech at the 47th SEACEN Governors'

Conference, Seoul, Korea, 13 February 2012. Our definition is wider as it also takes into account issues related with the channels of transmission of monetary policy.

16 Benjamin Braun, 'Central Banking and the Infrastructural Power of Finance: The Case of ECB Support for Repo and Securitization Markets', *Socio-Economic Review*, 2018. Advance online publication: doi:10.1093/ser/mwy008.

17 Daniela Gabor, 'A Step Too Far? The European Financial Transactions Tax on Shadow Banking', *Journal of European Public Policy* 23, no. 6 (2016): 925–45.

18 Manmohan Singh, 'Managing the Fed's Liftoff and Transmission of Monetary Policy', SSRN Scholarly Paper, Rochester, NY, Social Science Research Network, 1 September 2015.

19 Bank of England and European Central Bank, 'The Case for a Better Functioning Securitisation Market in the European Union', May 2014, www.ecb. europa.eu/pub/pdf/other/ecb-boe_case_better_funct ioning_securitisation_marketen.pdf.

20 Philippine Cour-Thimann, 'Monetary Policy and Redistribution: Information from Central Bank Balance Sheets in the Euro Area and the US', *Review of Economics* 64, no. 3 (2013): 293–324.

21 Holger Steltzner and Stefan Ruhkamp, 'Interview with Mario Draghi, President of the ECB', *Frankfurter Allgemeine Zeitung*, 24 February 2012.

22 Mario Draghi, 'Hearing at the Committee on Economic and Monetary Affairs', European

Parliament, 14 July 2014, www.ecb.europa.eu/press/key/date/2014/html/sp140714.en.html.

23 Lawrence Jacobs and Desmond King, *Fed Power: How Finance Wins* (Oxford: Oxford University Press, 2016).

24 Eric Helleiner, *The Status Quo Crisis: Global Financial Governance After the 2008 Meltdown* (Oxford: Oxford University Press, 2014).

25 In a further irony, three years before the crisis, Fed policy makers anticipated that they would face a short-term commitment problem to respect the Bagehot rule if a TBTF institution was to collapse. See Gary H. Stern and Ron J. Feldman, *Too Big to Fail: The Hazards of Bank Bailouts* (Washington DC: Brookings Institution Press, 2004).

Chapter 4 Central Banking Expertise

1 US Senate, 'Federal Reserve's Second Monetary Policy Report for 2002', Committee on Banking, Housing and Urban Affairs, United States Senate, 2002, 2, https://catalog.hathitrust.org/Record/003831882.

2 Energy derivatives were at the centre of the California energy crisis at the time. Later in the same Senate Committee Hearing, Greenspan reiterated his view: 'I continue to oppose legislation providing for additional regulation of energy derivatives [. . .].' Ibid., 50.

3 Interview material quoted in Fontan, 'Frankenstein in Europe'.

4 Prominent central bankers recognise that the com-

munity was wrong on this count – for instance: Committee on Oversight and Government Reform, 'The Financial Crisis and the Role of Federal Regulators', House of Representatives, Washington DC: US Government Printing Office, 23 October 2008; Carney, 'One Mission. One Bank'.

5 Christian Andersen, 'The Emperor's New Clothes' (1949 translation by Jean Hersholt), H.C. Andersen Centre, www.andersen.sdu.dk/vaerk/hersholt/The EmperorsNewClothes_e.html.

6 This framework is influenced by a long tradition going as far back as Socrates' maieutics, through John Stuart Mill's intellectualist argument for political liberty in John Stuart Mill, *On Liberty* (J.W. Parker and Son, 1859) and the 'norms of science' of Robert K. Merton, 'The Normative Structure of Science', in *The Sociology of Science: Theoretical and Empirical Investigations*, ed. Norman W. Storer (Chicago: University of Chicago Press, 1973), 267–78, leading to more recent propositions such as Helen Longino's 'procedural objectivity' in *Science as Social Knowledge* (Princeton: Princeton University Press, 1990).

7 Longino, *Science as Social Knowledge*.

8 Scott E. Page, *The Difference: How the Power of Diversity Creates Better Groups, Firms, Schools, and Societies*, new edition (Princeton: Princeton University Press, 2008); Kristen Intemann, 'Why Diversity Matters: Understanding and Applying the Diversity Component of the National Science Foundation's Broader Impacts Criterion', *Social Epistemology* 23, nos. 3–4 (1 July 2009): 249–66.

9 Committee on Finance and Industry, *Minutes of Evidence, Volume I* (London: HMSO, 1931), 30–1.

10 For discussions of the transition to transparency in the 1990s, see Nergiz N. Dincer and Barry Eichengreen, 'Central Bank Transparency: Where, Why, and With What Effects?', in *Central Banks as Economic Institutions*, ed. Jean-Philippe Touffut (Cheltenham: Edward Elgar Publishing, 2008), 391–406; Nicolas Jabko, 'Transparency and Accountability', in *Central Banks in the Age of the Euro: Europeanization, Convergence and Power*, ed. Kenneth H.F. Dyson and Martin Marcussen (Oxford: Oxford University Press, 2009), 391–406.

11 Alan S. Blinder, *The Quiet Revolution: Central Banking Goes Modern* (New Haven: Yale University Press, 2004), chap. 1.

12 European Central Bank, 'Transparency', 2017, www.ecb.europa.eu/ecb/orga/transparency/html/index.en.html.

13 The transcripts of the Federal Open Market Committee in the US are released after five years. The Bank of England accepted in late 2014 to release the transcripts of the policy meetings of its Monetary Policy Committee with an eight-year delay, but not to release the deliberation meetings of the same committee, based on suggestions from the Warsh report: Kevin Warsh, 'Transparency and the Bank of England's Monetary Policy Committee', London: Bank of England, December 2014, www.bankofengland.co.uk/-/media/boe/files/news/2014/december/tran

sparency-and-the-boes-mpc-review-by-kevin-warsh.
pdf. For the official response by the Bank: Bank of
England, 'Transparency and Accountability at the
Bank of England', 11 December 2014, www.ba
nkofengland.co.uk/-/media/boe/files/news/2014/dec
ember/transparency-and-the-boes-mpc-response.pdf.

14 Issing et al., *Monetary Policy in the Euro Area*, 69.
Many examples of information control could be
provided, e.g., the ECB's lack of transparency on
the list of companies benefiting from its corporate
bond-buying programme (Chapter 2).

15 Note that one argument for keeping deliberations of
policy meetings relatively secretive emphasises the
dynamics of criticism generation internal to the committee: the worry is that 'broadcasting the monthly
meetings of the [committee] live on television [. . .]
runs the risk of quashing the genuine deliberation
that is an essential feature of sound policymaking'.
Warsh, 'Transparency and the Bank of England's
Monetary Policy Committee', 5.

16 Martin Marcussen, 'Scientization of Central Banking:
The Politics of A-Politicization', in *Central Banks in
the Age of the Euro: Europeanization, Convergence,
and Power*, ed. Kenneth Dyson and Martin
Marcussen (Oxford: Oxford University Press, 2009),
373–90.

17 Lawrence H. White, 'The Federal Reserve System's
Influence on Research in Monetary Economics',
Econ Journal Watch 2, no. 2 (2005): 329.

18 For more information on the extent of the Fed's
research firepower, see White, 'The Federal Reserve

System's Influence on Research in Monetary Economics'; Ryan Grim, 'Priceless: How the Federal Reserve Bought the Economics Profession', *Huffington Post*, 23 October 2009; Peter Conti-Brown, *The Power and Independence of the Federal Reserve* (Princeton: Princeton University Press, 2016), chap. 4.

19 The numbers in 1993 have been reported to the US Congress by Greenspan; see Grim, 'Priceless'. The numbers for 2003 are from White, 'The Federal Reserve System's Influence on Research in Monetary Economics'. The numbers for 2017 are from our own calculations (websites accessed on 14 June and 30 October 2017 by two independent coders, the numbers being an average of the two counts).

20 Charles Freedman et al., 'External Evaluation of the Directorate General Research of the European Central Bank', European Central Bank, 25 January 2011, 51, www.ecb.europa.eu/pub/pdf/other/ecbrese archevaluationfinalen.pdf.

21 Mark Carney, 'Opening Remarks of the One Bank Research Agenda: Launch Conference', Bank of England, 25 February 2015, www.bankofengland.co. uk/-/media/boe/files/speech/2015/one-bank-research-agenda-launch-conference.pdf.

22 Ibid.

23 European Central Bank, 'Why Does the ECB Conduct Research?', European Central Bank, 28 September 2016, www.ecb.europa.eu/explainers/tell-me-more/ html/research.en.html.

24 Stephanie L. Mudge and Antoine Vauchez, 'Fielding

Supranationalism: The European Central Bank as a Field Effect', *The Sociological Review Monographs* 64, no. 2 (1 March 2016): 146–69. For similar claims about the Fed, see Martin M.G. Fase and Wim F.V. Vanthoor, *The Federal Reserve System Discussed: A Comparative Analysis*, SUERF Studies, no. 10 (Vienna: Société universitaire européenne de recherches financières, 2000); and Grim, 'Priceless'. For even more serious claims of censure about more distant events, see Robert D. Auerbach, *Deception and Abuse at the Fed: Henry B. Gonzales Battles Alan Greenspan's Bank* (Austin: University of Texas Press, 2008).

25 Conti-Brown, *The Power and Independence of the Federal Reserve*, 92.

26 Our own calculations based on the CV of each board member. Grim, in 'Priceless', reached a similar figure in 2009.

27 See, in ibid., how Robert King, then editor in chief of the *Journal of Monetary Economics*, and Stephen Williamson – still senior associate editor – dismiss the hypothesis that Fed connections affect the content of the journal.

28 Our own calculations based on the papers referenced in the Bank for International Settlements, Central Bank Research Hub – Homepage, 2017, www.bis.org/cbhub. The titles and abstracts of papers have been systematically searched using a keyword list expanded up to the point of saturation. The identified papers have then been manually classified.

29 Christopher Adolph, *Bankers, Bureaucrats, and Central Bank Politics: The Myth of Neutrality* (New York: Cambridge University Press, 2013).

30 Kenneth Haar, 'Open Door for Forces of Finance at the ECB', Corporate Europe Observatory, October 2017, https://corporateeurope.org/sites/default/files/attachments/open_door_for_forces_of_finance_report.pdf.

31 Neil Fligstein et al. 'Seeing Like the Fed: Culture, Cognition, and Framing in the Failure to Anticipate the Financial Crisis of 2008', *American Sociological Review* 82, no. 5 (2017): 879–909.

32 WSJ Pro, 'Transcript: Fed Officials Meet With Fed Up Activists at Jackson Hole', *Wall Street Journal*, 26 August 2016.

33 Interview by Reuters cited in Auerbach, *Deception and Abuse at the Fed*, 143.

Chapter 5 Whither Central Banking? Institutional Options for the Future

1 Charles Goodhart, 'The Changing Role of Central Banks', *Financial History Review* 18, no. 02 (August 2011): 135–54.

2 Fontan, Claveau and Dietsch, 'Central Banking and Inequalities', 342–3.

3 Frank van Lerven, 'A Guide to Public Money Creation', Positive Money, May 2016, positivemoney.org.

4 Andrew Sheng, 'Central Banks Can and Should Do Their Part in Funding Sustainability', UNEP Inquiry,

June 2015, http://unepinquiry.org/publication/cen
tral-banks-funding-sustainability.

5 Mark Blyth and Eric Lonergan, 'Print Less but Transfer More: Why Central Banks Should Give Money Directly to the People', *Foreign Affairs* 93 (2014): 98.

6 See 'Fed Up: The National Campaign for a Strong Economy. Powered by the Center for Popular Democracy and Action For the Common Good', 2016, http://whatrecovery.org.

7 Milton Friedman, *The Optimum Quantity of Money* (New Jersey: Transaction Publishers, 2005).

8 Romain Baeriswyl, 'The Case for the Separation of Money and Credit', in *Monetary Policy, Financial Crises, and the Macroeconomy*, ed. Frank Heinemann, Ulrich Klüh and Sebastian Watzka (Dordrecht: Springer Berlin Heidelberg, 2017).

9 See the preface to the 1982 edition in Milton Friedman, *Capitalism and Freedom* (Chicago: University of Chicago Press, 2009 [1962]), xiv.

10 Crouch, *The Strange Non-Death of Neo-Liberalism*; Jacob Hacker and Paul Pierson, *Winner-Take-All Politics: How Washington Made the Rich Richer – And Turned its Back on the Middle Class* (New York: Simon and Schuster, 2010).